WOMEN ATHLETES WHO RULE!

By *Elizabeth McGarr McCue*

Sports Illustrated KIDS

Writer Elizabeth McGarr McCue
Editor Mark Bechtel
Designer Drew Dzwonkowski
Photo Editor Abby Nicolas
Reporter Jeremy Fuchs
Copy Editor Pamela Roberts
Production Manager Hillary Leary

Copyright © 2018 Time Inc. Books

Published by Liberty Street,
an imprint of Time Inc. Books,
a division of Meredith Corporation
225 Liberty Street
New York, NY 10281

ISBN: 978-1-68330-073-1
Library of Congress Control Number:
2017963815

First edition, 2018
1 QGV 18
10 9 8 7 6 5 4 3 2 1

We welcome your comments and
suggestions about Time Inc. Books.

Time Inc. Books
Attention: Book Editors
P.O. Box 62310
Tampa, FL 33662-2310
(800) 765-6400

timeincbooks.com

Time Inc. Books products may be purchased for
business or promotional use. For information on
bulk purchases, please contact Christi Crowley in
the Special Sales Department at (845) 895-9858.

WOMEN ATHLETES WHO RULE!

▶ The history of sports is long on tales of heroic baseball players, football stars, and NBA legends. But what about the accomplishments of fearless, phenomenal female athletes? Too often they are minimized, marginalized, or simply ignored. The women we included in this book are extraordinary athletes who all shaped the narratives of their sports. Their stories—on and off the field—will inspire anyone who truly appreciates awesomeness in athletics.

CONTENTS

1.

PERSTARS

These athletes reinvented what it means to be a sports celebrity

Which female skier has the most Alpine World Cup victories?

When she was only two, **Lindsey Vonn** was up on skis for the first time. By 16, she had made the U.S. Ski Team. Four years later, she won her first World Cup race, and at 24, she became the first U.S. woman in a quarter of a century to win the overall World Cup title. She then became the first American woman to win Olympic gold in the downhill and also took bronze in the Super-G at the 2010 Games and bronze in the downhill in 2018. Through the end of the 2017–18 season she had 82 wins, more than any female World Cup racer and trailing only Sweden's Ingemar Stenmark (86).

Vonn has had her share of crashes over the years and has sustained numerous serious injuries, including one that forced her to miss the 2014 Olympics. But the same tenacity that has pushed her to attack challenging race courses has also allowed her to return to the slopes after each mishap.

FAST FACT:
Vonn's 20 crystal globes (the award given for World Cup points titles in individual disciplines and overall) are the most for any skier.

Who has been named FIFA World Player of the Year more than anyone?

Some athletes win wherever they go. **Marta** is one of those people. From 2005 through 2015, while playing for clubs in Sweden, Brazil, and the U.S., she led her teams to league championships in every year but one, winning FIFA World Player of the Year five times in a row beginning in 2006. As a striker for Brazil's national team, Marta received the Golden Ball (top player) and Golden Boot (top scorer) at the 2007 World Cup, during which she led Brazil to its first final. She also helped her country win back-to-back silver medals at the 2004 and 2008 Olympics, and was one of eight athletes who carried the Olympic flag at the 2016 Games, which Brazil hosted. Born Marta Vieira da Silva, she has more international goals (104) than fellow Brazilian Péle, who is often called the greatest soccer player of all time.

WOW FACTOR

15

Goals Marta has scored in four World Cup appearances, a record.

Which singles player has the most Grand Slam titles in the Open era?

WOW FACTOR

14

Number of doubles Grand Slams she and sister Venus have won together. They are 14–0.

She won her first Grand Slam event, the 1999 U.S. Open, when she was only 17 years old. **Serena Williams** has now won more major tournaments (23) than any tennis player since professionals were first allowed to participate in them, in 1968. To go along with her six victories at the U.S. Open, she has seven at the Australian Open, three at the French Open, and seven at Wimbledon. In 2003 and 2015, she completed what became known as the Serena Slam, winning four major tournaments in a row (a little different than a true Grand Slam, which entails four wins in a calendar year). "I do want to be known as the greatest ever," she said in 2015.

It's hard to argue that she's not already. Since first topping the world rankings in 2002, she has been number one for 319 weeks, including 186 in a row.

After she won the 2017 Australian Open—seven matches in straight sets—while pregnant with her daughter, Alexis, Williams ascended to the top spot again. At 35, she was the oldest number one in history.

FAST FACT:
Williams has worked in fashion since 2003, when she debuted her first clothing line. Her sister Venus has a line as well.

" The success of every woman should be the inspiration to another. **We should raise each other up.** Make sure you're very courageous. Be strong, be extremely kind, and above all, be humble."

—in 2015, at the Glamour Women of the Year Awards

FAST FACT:
Walsh Jennings, who has four Olympic medals, is the most decorated beach volleyball Olympian ever.

Who has won the most beach volleyball tournaments of all time?

She may have begun her career playing indoors, but the 6'3" **Kerri Walsh Jennings** made her name on the soft sand of the world's beach volleyball courts. A four-time All-America for Stanford's NCAA indoor team, she played for the U.S. at the 2000 Olympics. The next year, she joined Misty May-Treanor on the pro beach international tour (FIVB) and then on the U.S. circuit, the AVP Tour. Together the duo earned five consecutive AVP Team of the Year awards (2003 through 2007), three straight FIVB world championships (2005, 2007, and 2009), and three Olympic gold medals (2004, 2008, 2012).

After May-Treanor retired, Walsh Jennings partnered with April Ross; they won 11 of the 32 international tournaments they entered and snagged bronze at the 2016 Olympics. That year, Walsh Jennings became the first U.S. woman to win 600 international matches. She's taken first at 133 tournaments, making her the winningest women's beach player in history.

Who beat her famous brother to the basketball Hall of Fame by 17 years?

When she arrived at USC in 1982, **Cheryl Miller** had just led Riverside (California) Polytechnic High to a 132–4 record over four years. She also held state marks for points in a career (3,405) and a season (1,156). And yet, she said at the time, "I don't consider myself a superstar."

When she graduated from USC, there was no doubt in *anyone's* mind just how extraordinary she was: The three-time Naismith Player of the Year and four-time All-America had led the Trojans to two NCAA championships and Team USA to gold at the 1984 Olympics. Miller hustled and she had style, and she grabbed offensive rebounds better than anyone. Younger brother Reggie was no slouch either: He was a five-time All-Star in 18 years with the Indiana Pacers. Cheryl was inducted into the Naismith Memorial Basketball Hall of Fame in 1995; Reggie made it in 2012.

WOW FACTOR

105

Points Miller scored in a game as a high school senior, second most in history.

FAST FACT:
A four-year starter for the UCLA women's basketball team, she scored 1,167 points and led the Bruins in rebounding as a senior (9.1 per game).

" As an athlete trying to be the very best, **winning one gold medal wasn't enough.** Once I won one, then I had to work even harder."

—in 2000, at DePauw University's commencement

Who has held the world record in the heptathlon since 1988?

To succeed at the heptathlon, a seven-event track and field competition, one needs to be well-rounded. **Jackie Joyner-Kersee** was well-rounded, all right. At the 1988 Olympics, four years after coming in second by a mere five points, she broke her own world record, with 7,291 points, grabbing a gold to add to her silver. (She also won the long jump in 1988, then nabbed bronze in 1992 and 1996.)

At the 1992 Games in Barcelona, Joyner-Kersee didn't match her record. (In 30 years, no one has.) But she did repeat as the gold medalist in the event. She ended her career with two world championships each in the long jump and the heptathlon.

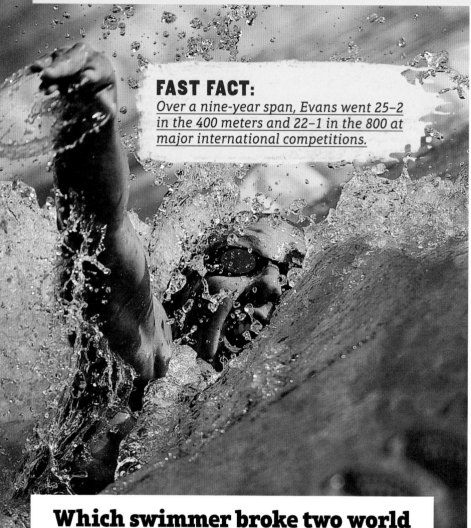

FAST FACT:
Over a nine-year span, Evans went 25–2 in the 400 meters and 22–1 in the 800 at major international competitions.

Which softball star struck out Major League Baseball sluggers?

A two-time collegiate player of the year, **Jennie Finch** won a record 60 straight games for Arizona, leading the Wildcats to victory at the 2001 Women's College World Series. She was 4–0 in Olympic outings and pitched 19 scoreless innings to help the U.S. win gold at the 2004 Games and silver in 2008. Her pitches reached 70 miles per hour. Just how dominant did that make her? Well, major leaguers Brian Giles, Mike Piazza, Albert Pujols, and Alex Rodriguez all struck out against her.

Which swimmer broke two world records when she was 15 years old?

B efore she began her junior year at El Dorado High in California in 1987, 15-year-old freestyle swimmer **Janet Evans** had already finished the 800- and 1,500-meter races faster than anyone in history. That winter, she set the world record in the 400 meters. As a 17-year-old senior, she took the 1988 Olympics by storm, breaking her own world record in the 400 and also winning the 800 meters and the 400 individual medley. (She defended her 800 title in 1992.)

Her best time in the 800 (8:16.22) stood as the world record from 1989 until Rebecca Adlington of Great Britain, who was born in 1989, beat it at the 2008 Games.

Who was the first female basketball player to get her own signature shoe line?

She was a big enough deal to have a Nike sneaker named after her—and that was *before* **Sheryl Swoopes** won three Olympic gold medals, three WNBA MVP awards, and four straight WNBA championships with the Houston Comets from 1997 through 2000.

The top girls' high school player in Texas, Swoopes went on to win the 1993 NCAA championship at Texas Tech, where she set eight school records, including the single-game mark for points (53). In 2016, she became the first Red Raider, man or woman, to be inducted into the basketball Hall of Fame.

WOW FACTOR

47

Points Swoopes scored for Texas Tech in the 1993 NCAA title game, a championship record for men and women.

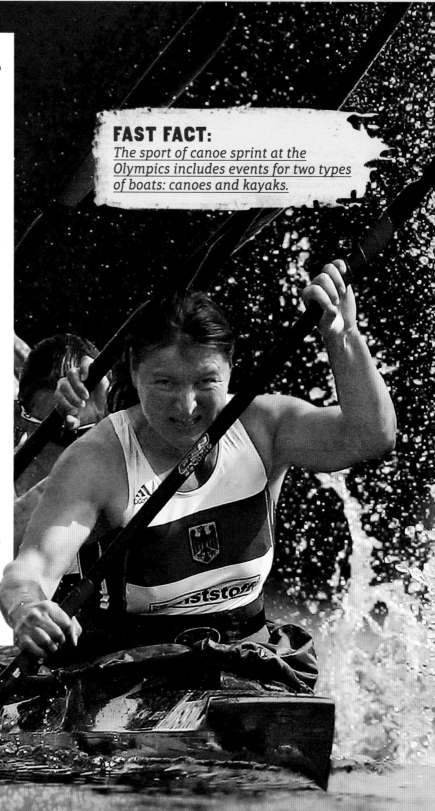

Who was both the youngest and oldest Olympic kayaking champion?

FAST FACT:
The sport of canoe sprint at the Olympics includes events for two types of boats: canoes and kayaks.

By the time 42-year-old **Birgit Fischer** of Germany left the 2004 Olympics in Athens, her sixth Games, she had earned a total of eight gold medals and four silvers, more than any kayaker and tied for the second most ever by a female Olympian. Her victory in Athens made her the oldest kayaker to win a gold medal—24 years after she first entered the record books. At the 1980 Games, she had became the youngest kayaker to win gold, when she was just 18.

Over the years she won gold in K1, K2, and K4 (one, two, and four rowers). At all world championships held from 1981 through 1987, she swept the 500-meter K1, K2, and K4 races except in 1986, when she took time off to have a baby.

Which skater won 10 world championships and starred in 11 movies?

Already the children's figure skating champion of Oslo, Norway, at eight years old, **Sonja Henie** went on to become one of the biggest celebrities of her time. She is still considered one of the greatest performers in her sport. Henie won the championship of Norway in 1923 and skated in the inaugural Winter Olympics, in 1924, when she was only 11. She then won three consecutive Olympic golds (1928, 1932, 1936) and 10 straight world singles championships (1927 through 1936), feats no woman or man has equaled since.

She turned professional in 1936, touring the U.S. with her Hollywood Ice Revue. She also starred in feature films, the first of which, *One in a Million*, was released late that year.

FAST FACT:
As a child, Henie studied ballet with a teacher who had instructed Anna Pavlova, the most famous ballerina of all time.

Who was the U.S. Soccer Female Player of the Year five years in a row?

When she was 15, **Mia Hamm** became the youngest person to play for the U.S. national team. When she retired in 2004, she was the organization's all-time leading scorer (158 goals, since passed by Abby Wambach) and was first in the world in international appearances (276, now third).

In between, she won two collegiate player of the year awards and helped the University of North Carolina juggernaut win four NCAA titles. She led the country in scoring in 1990, then set the collegiate record for points in a season (97) in 1992.

Hamm played in four World Cups (helping the U.S. win in 1991 and 1999) and three Olympics (leading the U.S. to gold in 1996 and 2004). She was, quite simply, the face of women's soccer in the country when it was gaining momentum in the early 1990s. Hamm earned U.S. Soccer Female Player of the Year honors from 1994 through 1998.

DID YOU KNOW?

The U.S. women's national team didn't form until 1985, even though the men's team had been around since 1916. There was no World Cup for women until 1991, and the sport wasn't in the Olympics until 1996. (Men's soccer has been an Olympic sport since 1900.) Hamm (*above left*, with Michelle Akers) was on the U.S. squads that won gold at both of those inaugural women's tournaments.

WOW FACTOR

145

Career assists Hamm had in international play, a U.S. record.

Which speedskater won the same race in three straight Olympics?

At the 1992 Olympics in Albertville, France, skater **Bonnie Blair** won the 500 meters to become the first woman to win that race at back-to-back Games. She also became the first American Winter Olympian to win consecutive titles in any sport—much to the delight of the 45 family members in the crowd who serenaded her with "My Bonnie Lies Over the Ocean." Blair added gold in the 1,000 that year, then won both events at the next Winter Games, in 1994, ending her career with more golds than any American Winter Olympian. That December, SPORTS ILLUSTRATED named her and fellow speedskater Johann Olav Koss its Sportspeople of the Year.

WOW FACTOR

6

Olympic medals Blair won (five gold, one bronze), the most by a female U.S. Winter Olympian.

Who was the first American woman to win an Olympic medal in judo?

She thought she wouldn't make the 2004 Olympics, so high school judoist **Ronda Rousey** named her cat Beijing, the site of the 2008 Games. Well, 17-year-old Rousey made the team in 2004 (she was eliminated early) and again in 2008, winning bronze in the 63-to-70-kg class to become the first American judoist to medal in an Olympics. Over the next decade, she became a Mixed Martial Arts superstar, defending her Ultimate Fighting Championship title six times.

Who shot the lowest round in LPGA tour history?

When she tapped in for par on the 18th hole of her second round at the 2001 Standard Register Ping tournament, **Annika Sorenstam** of Sweden jumped into her caddie's arms. "I'm absolutely overwhelmed," she said. "I can't believe what I just did." That par putt meant she had shot a round of 59, a first on the LPGA tour. Two days later, she set another record by finishing at 27 under par to clinch a victory, one of 72 she racked up over a 15-year career. She won back-to-back U.S. Opens (1995, 1996) and retired with 10 major championship wins, tied with Babe Didrikson Zaharias for fourth most all time.

At the 2003 Colonial, Sorenstam may not have made the cut, but she became the first woman to play with men on the PGA Tour since Zaharias did it (for the second time) in 1945.

21

Which member of the Final Five has a gymnastics move named after her?

You know you've made an impact on a sport when you influence the way your fellow athletes train and perform. **Simone Biles** inserted a tumbling pass into her floor exercise routine: a double flip in layout position (straight body) with a half twist and a front landing, which is more difficult than a backward landing. The move was called the Biles, after the woman who perfected it.

If Biles wasn't perfect at the 2016 Olympics, she was close, winning gold in the all-around, floor exercise, and on the balance beam; earning bronze in the vault; and leading the U.S. to gold in the team event.

Her performance at the Games came on the heels of an unprecedented three straight world championships and four consecutive U.S. titles in the all-around.

The Texas native happened into the sport during a field trip to a local gym when she was six. Her future coach, Aimee Boorman, knew Biles was special from the start. Recalled Boorman, "She had better balance on her hands than the other girls did on their feet. She'd have a conversation and hold a handstand at the same time."

DID YOU KNOW?

This pint-sized champion was a pretty big deal after the 2016 Olympics. She was on *Dancing with the Stars*, made the rounds on the talk shows, and had a cameo on the Nickelodeon show *Mutt & Stuff*. Biles also joined fellow Olympians at the White House, where the 4'8" gymnast met 5'11" Michelle Obama.

WOW FACTOR

10

World championship medals Biles has won, a record.

Rio2016 ⬤⬤⬤⬤⬤

FAST FACT:
Ladewig was reportedly so fast as a kid that she wasn't allowed to participate in end-of-season races at local playgrounds.

What grandmother of five was named Bowler of the Year a record ninth time in 1963?

n 1955, SPORTS ILLUSTRATED called **Marion Ladewig** "the greatest woman bowler of all time." She had just won five straight U.S. Women's Opens. Her career was far from over, though. She won the tournament three more times and retired with nine Bowler of the Year awards and a record five World's Invitational titles, the last of which she earned in 1965.

A recreational softball player, Ladewig took up bowling when she was 22 only because her friends were into the sport. She put on exhibitions in Europe, Australia, and Asia, and even bowled on the lanes in the White House.

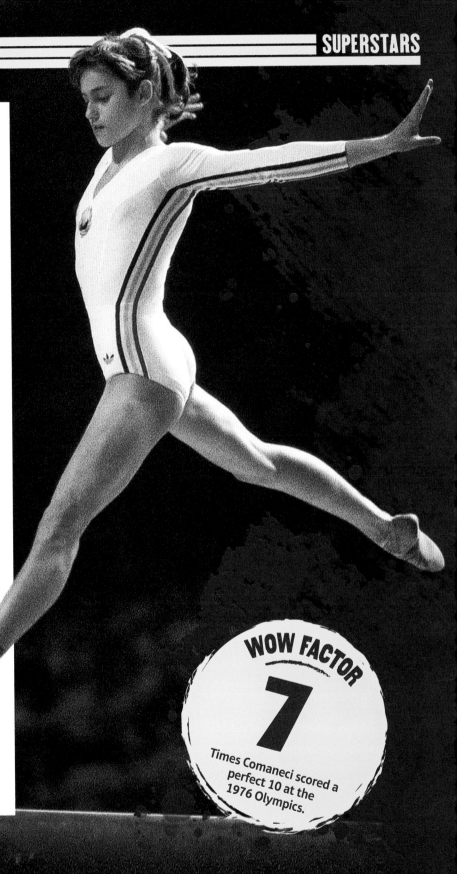

Who was the first gymnast to score a perfect 10?

When **Nadia Comaneci** of Romania finished her uneven bars routine at the 1976 Olympics, she looked up at the scoreboard and saw "1.00." That wasn't how many points she had lost on her routine—the scoreboard just wasn't equipped to display a perfect 10. And for good reason: No gymnast had ever earned one. Not only did she win gold in the uneven bars that year, but she also won the all-around and the beam competition, took silver with her team, and won bronze in the floor exercise. She then repeated as the gold medalist on the beam and uneven bars at the 1980 Games and took silver in the all-around.

Her coach, Bela Karolyi, went on to mentor future Olympic gold medalists for the U.S. Said Karolyi after Comaneci's performance in 1976, "She has three qualities. The physical qualities—strength, speed, agility. The intellectual qualities— intelligence and the power to concentrate. And . . . Nadia has courage."

WOW FACTOR

7

Times Comaneci scored a perfect 10 at the 1976 Olympics.

Who is the most decorated woman in U.S. Olympic track and field history?

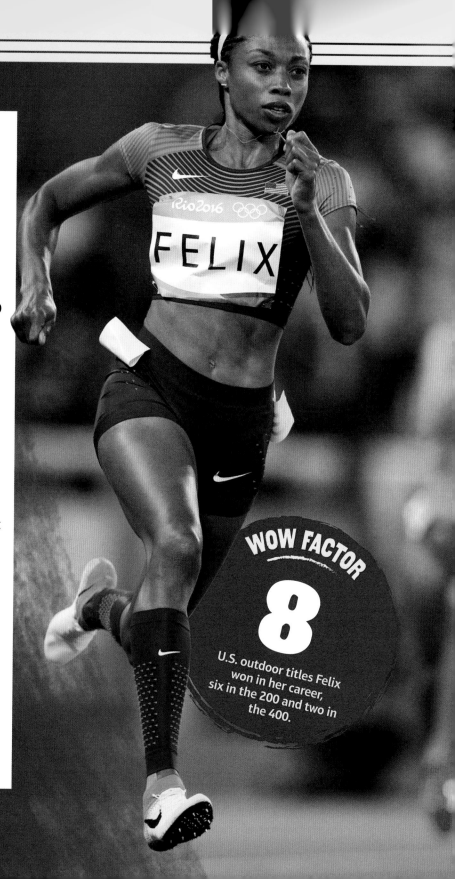

She lost the 400-meter race at the 2016 Olympics by .07 of a second, but when sprinter **Allyson Felix** stepped off the podium that day with her silver medal, she had collected more Olympic hardware than any American woman in her sport. Her ninth medal tied her with Merlene Ottey-Page of Jamaica for the women's track and field record. Felix had won gold in the 4 × 400 relay (twice), the 200, and the 4 × 100 relay; and she had taken silver in the 200 (twice). The following summer, she won her 16th world championship medal to become the most decorated athlete at the event.

Felix enjoyed early international success at 100 meters, winning gold at the World Youth Championships when she was 15. She then broke the national high school record in the 200 during her senior year.

WOW FACTOR

8

U.S. outdoor titles Felix won in her career, six in the 200 and two in the 400.

Who is the only tennis player to win all four majors and Olympic gold in the same year?

t's known as the Golden Slam, and **Steffi Graf** is the only person who has ever accomplished it. She began the 1988 season with a victory in the Australian Open (against future Hall of Famer Chris Evert), then won the French Open, Wimbledon (against future Hall of Famer Martina Navratilova), the U.S. Open, and the Olympics singles tournament before the year was over.

The native of Germany held the record for most career Grand Slam singles victories in the Open era (22) until Serena Williams broke it in 2017. Graf also topped the world rankings for a record 186 straight weeks, a mark she now shares with Williams.

FAST FACT:
Graf married U.S. tennis star Andre Agassi in 2001. They have won 30 Grand Slam tournaments between them.

2.

WONDER WOMEN

Some athletes have the power to transcend sports and create seismic shifts in our culture

DID YOU KNOW?

In 1998 and 1999, Wickenheiser was invited to the Philadelphia Flyers' NHL rookie camp. And when her shot found the back of the net in a February 2003 game for Kirkkonummen Salamat in Finland, Wickenheiser became the first woman to score a goal in men's professional hockey.

FAST FACT:
Wickenheiser was the flag bearer for the Canadian Olympic team at the opening ceremony of the 2014 Olympics in Sochi.

Which hockey superstar competed in both the Summer and Winter Olympics?

Before retiring in 2017, **Hayley Wickenheiser** was considered the greatest female hockey player in the world. She had certainly earned the title. In 1994, the native of Shaunovon, Saskatchewan, led Team Canada to the first of seven IHHF women's world championships, and she won four Olympic hockey gold medals and one silver.

At the 2000 Summer Games, she played for Canada's softball team to become the second Canadian woman to compete in both the Summer and Winter Olympics and the first to do it in a team sport. Wickenheiser is the all-time Olympic hockey leader in points (51).

Who was the first woman to drive in the Indianapolis 500 and the Daytona 500?

They are the two most prestigious events in American racing, and during a three-month stretch in 1977, **Janet Guthrie** became the first woman to compete in both. First came the Daytona 500, where Guthrie came in 12th and was the race's top rookie. At the Indy 500, Guthrie didn't fare as well, finishing only 27 laps, but in 1978 she was ninth.

Her sixth-place finish at Bristol Motor Speedway in 1977 was the best by a woman in a NASCAR race until Danica Patrick tied it in 2014.

In Guthrie's autobiography, she recounts that life on the track was difficult because so many people did not accept her. And her career effectively ended in 1980 because she could not get sponsors to pay for her car. "If I contributed some small bit to the changing perception of women's abilities, I am glad of that," she wrote. "It was not the reason I did what I did. I drove race cars because I could not do otherwise; because it was an obsession and a passion."

Who was the first woman to play pro baseball?

She played in men's amateur leagues until she was 60 years old, but it was the two seasons she played in the Negro leagues, for the Indianapolis Clowns and the Kansas City Monarchs in the early 1950s, that earned **Toni Stone** a spot in the history books.

The first woman to play professional baseball with men grew up in St. Paul, Minnesota, which recognized her by declaring March 6, 1990, Marcenia Toni Stone Alberga Day. In 1997, one year after she died, a baseball field at a sports complex in St. Paul was dedicated in her honor.

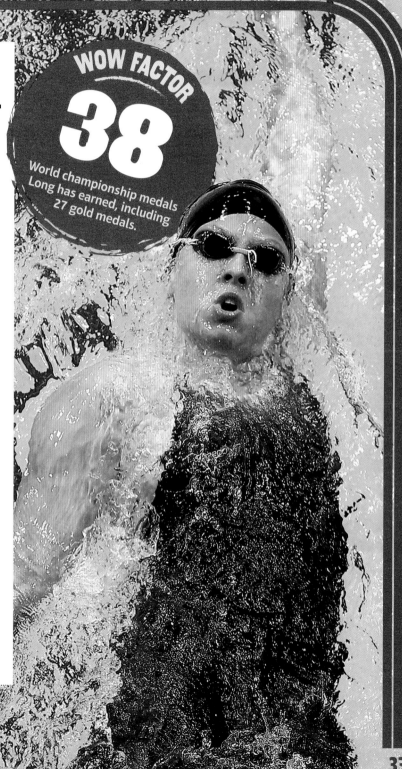

Which swimmer won three gold medals at the Paralympics when she was only 12?

Born without parts of her lower legs, **Jessica Long** was adopted from a Russian orphanage when she was 13 months old. Before she was two, she had both legs amputated below the knee. She began swimming competitively when she was 10 and made a splash at the 2004 Paralympics, winning three gold medals. Two years later, at the 2006 Paralympic world championships, she broke five world records and won nine—nine!—gold medals. The following spring, Long became the first Paralympian to win the Sullivan Award, which is given to the top amateur athlete in the U.S.

Through the 2016 Games, Long had won 23 total medals to become the second-most-decorated U.S. Paralympian in history.

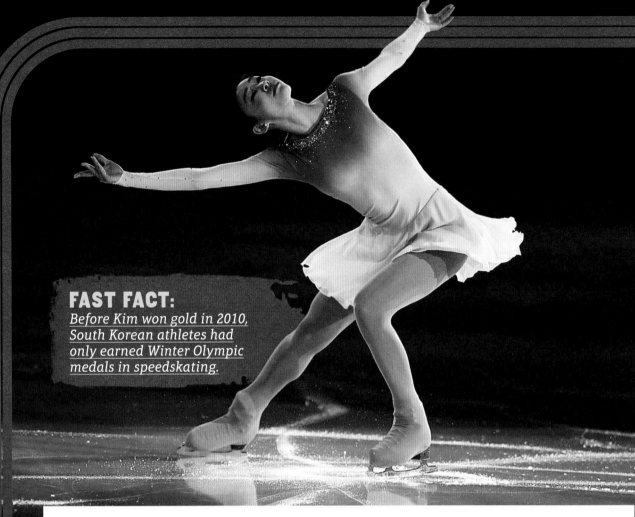

Who was the first South Korean figure skater to win an Olympic medal?

Entering the 2010 Olympics, **Kim Yuna** had already won world championships at the junior and senior levels and was the favorite to win gold. She didn't let the fans down, setting points records in the short program, free skate, and combined score. TIME magazine named her one of the world's 100 most influential people that year.

Kim again wowed crowds at the 2013 world championships after taking two years off from international competition, winning by a whopping 21 points. Many thought she should have also won gold at the 2014 Olympics, where she instead took silver, behind Russian skater Adelina Sotnikova.

At the peak of her career, Kim was a superstar in South Korea, where she was known as Queen Yuna. Her photo was on billboards! As her country put together its ultimately successful bid to host the 2018 Olympics in PyeongChang, Kim was an influential part of the process, presenting to the International Olympic Committee. She then lit the cauldron at the opening ceremony.

Which tennis player has won the most matches in the Open era?

Over her professional tennis career, **Martina Navratilova** pretty much did it all. She won championships in singles (18 Grand Slams), doubles (31), and mixed doubles (10), the last of these titles coming in mixed doubles at the 2006 U.S. Open, when she was 49. Navratilova won 2,189 matches, more than any tennis player since 1968, when professionals began to compete.

She simply dominated the sport in the 1980s and was named the Associated Press Athlete of the Year in 1983 and 1986. Navratilova, who became a broadcaster after retiring, is also a vocal supporter of gay rights.

WOW FACTOR

9

Singles titles Navratilova won at Wimbledon, the most ever. Roger Federer is second on the list, with eight.

7

Wins Zaharias had on the LPGA tour after she was diagnosed with cancer in 1953.

Who was the greatest athlete of the first half of the 20th century?

The world has seen faster and stronger athletes since 1950, but no one in the last 100 years has been as multi-talented as **Babe Didrikson Zaharias.** When she returned home to Texas after taking gold in the javelin and the hurdles, and silver in the high jump at the 1932 Olympics, 10,000 people showed up at the airport to cheer for the 21-year-old phenom.

Didrikson excelled at every sport she tried. She took up golf seriously in her early 20s and won the U.S. and the British amateurs in 1946 and 1947, respectively. She was instrumental in the founding of the LPGA tour in 1950 and won 31 tournaments in six years.

She was a three-time Amateur Athletic Union All-America basketball player and led her team to a national title in 1931. And she was an all-star softball athlete who pitched in MLB exhibition games. To stay in tip-top shape, she used various methods of training, including boxing.

The day that she died of cancer at only 45, President Eisenhower said, "She ... won the admiration of every person in the United States, all sports people all over the world, and in her gallant fight against cancer, she put up one of the kind of fights that inspire us all."

FAST FACT: *At the 1932 national AAU track meet, Babe—by herself—won the team championship after taking first in five events, tying for first in one, and finishing fourth in another. The second-place team had 22 members.*

Who was nicknamed the Queen of Diving?

When she first began diving at the age of eight, **Fu Mingxia** didn't know how to swim. "My instructor had to pull me out of the pool with a piece of rope," she said before the 1996 Olympics. At those Games, Fu added to her collection of two world championships and an Olympic gold, defending her title in the 10-meter platform and also winning gold in the three-meter springboard. In 2000, she took gold in springboard again and silver in the springboard synchronized event, becoming the first female diver to win gold in three straight Olympics.

FAST FACT:
Fu won her first world championship when she was 12, and at 13 was the second-youngest athlete to ever win Olympic gold.

Who won world titles in two sports in the same year?

Let's just say that 1976 was a very good year for **Sheila Young Ochowicz.** At the Olympics in February, the speedskater won gold in the 500 meters, silver in the 1,500, and bronze in the 1,000. Then she won the world sprint speedskating championship. That summer, she took first at the world sprint-cycling championship. Over her career, she snagged three world championships in each sport. "You could say I'm a pretty competitive person," she said after that 1976 cycling title. "I like winning at things."

Who led Team USA to its first Olympic gold in women's basketball?

A plane crashed in **Lynette Woodard's** Kansas neighborhood, just missing her house, when she was five years old. The crash site eventually became a park where Woodard fell in love with basketball. "I was always looking for a chance to play," Woodard recalled later. "Soon guys were picking me before they picked their friends. Or I would be doing the picking."

By the time she graduated from the University of Kansas in 1981, she was the all-time leading scorer (3,649 points) in Division I women's history. Her strength, quickness, and leaping ability changed the way women's basketball, at the time a much slower game, was played. Woodard was captain of the 1984 squad that won Team USA's first Olympic gold in the sport.

FAST FACT:
Woodard played pro ball in Italy and Japan, and joined the WNBA for its first two seasons, in 1997 and 1998.

Who was the star of the U.S. Olympic volleyball team that won silver in 1984?

Leading up to the 1984 Olympics, SPORTS ILLUSTRATED called **Flo Hyman** "a phenomenal athlete who seemingly strikes the ball with enough ferocity to rearrange the grain in a wood floor." Wow. Indeed, the 6'5" Hyman, who had missed the Olympics in 1980 when the U.S. boycotted the Games, was one of the most powerful and graceful volleyball players of all time. She anchored the U.S. squad that was expected to win gold in 1984 but settled for silver. It was still the first-ever medal for Team USA.

Hyman was named Best Attacker at the 1981 World Cup and helped the U.S. win bronze at the 1982 world championships. She died when she was only 31, while playing a match in Japan. She had not known that she had been born with a genetic condition that had led to a heart problem.

WOW FACTOR

3

Seasons Hyman earned All-America honors in volleyball at the University of Houston.

FAST FACT: *Cuthbert carried the Olympic torch at the opening ceremony for the 2000 Olympics, which were held in Australia. Fellow sprint medalist Raelene Boyle pushed her wheelchair.*

Who was the first woman to win Olympic gold in four different events?

She set a world record in the 200-meter dash in 1956 when she was 18 years old, but **Betty Cuthbert** still didn't think she would make the team for that year's Olympics, which were being held in her native Australia. So she bought a ticket to attend the Games as a fan. Not only did Cuthbert make the team, but she also became a national hero and a world-famous track star after winning gold in the 100, the 200, and as part of the 4 × 100 relay team.

Though she left the 1960 Olympics empty-handed, she returned to the Games and won gold in the 400 meters in 1964, the first year the race was held for women.

In the late 1960s, Cuthbert was diagnosed with multiple sclerosis and over the next several decades was an advocate for those with the illness.

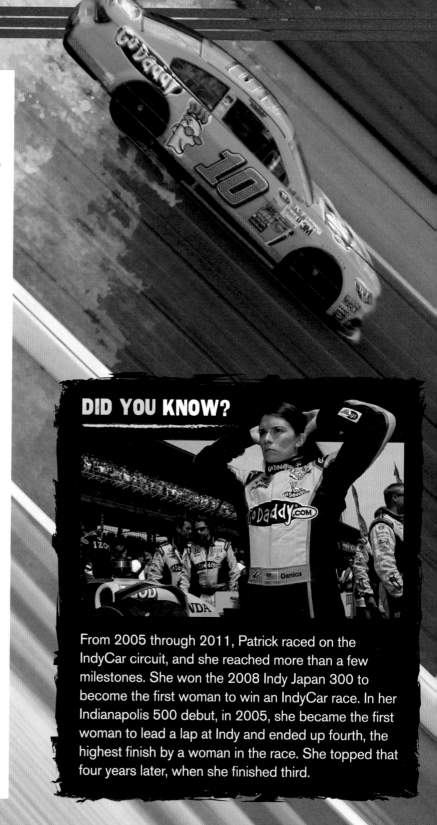

Who was the first woman to drive a full NASCAR Cup schedule?

She was already an accomplished open-wheel racer in IndyCar when **Danica Patrick** made her stock car debut in 2010 in one of NASCAR's lower circuits. "I had so much fun in the race car today," she said afterward. "I can't wait to do it again."

Patrick steadily moved up the ranks of the sport, advancing from the ARCA Racing Series to the Nationwide Series, and finally, to the Sprint Cup Series, NASCAR's top tier, in 2012. She ran 10 races that year, and in 2013 she ran 36 out of 36, the first time a woman had raced every event on the schedule.

In seven years of Cup racing, Patrick had seven top 10s but never averaged higher than 20th in points. Like Janet Guthrie before her, Patrick faced criticism from fellow drivers and from those who didn't think she belonged in NASCAR. "It's something that hasn't been uncommon for my entire career," she said in 2013. "It doesn't get to me. The haters are louder than the nice people, unfortunately."

DID YOU KNOW?

From 2005 through 2011, Patrick raced on the IndyCar circuit, and she reached more than a few milestones. She won the 2008 Indy Japan 300 to become the first woman to win an IndyCar race. In her Indianapolis 500 debut, in 2005, she became the first woman to lead a lap at Indy and ended up fourth, the highest finish by a woman in the race. She topped that four years later, when she finished third.

Which softball player also trained to be an orthopedic surgeon?

Softball only became an Olympic sport in 1996. By then **Dot Richardson** had helped Team USA win three world championships (1986, 1990, 1994) and three Pan-American Games. The Summer Olympics in Atlanta in 1996 was softball's big close-up, and Richardson and her teammates put on a show.

The three-time All-America at UCLA hit what would be the winning home run against China in that inaugural gold medal game. At the time, she had just finished medical school and was in the middle of a five-year stint at a hospital working in orthopedic surgery. The year after she finished, she helped Team USA win gold at the 2000 Olympics.

FAST FACT: *When she was 13, Richardson became the youngest athlete to play in the Women's Major Fastpitch national championship.*

Who stole 109 bases in 1946 to lead the All-American Girls Professional Baseball League?

Her local paper called her "a speed demon on the base paths." A former major league player referred to her as the "fanciest-fielding first baseman I've ever seen, man or woman."

In short, **Dorothy Kamenshek** could flat-out play ball. So during World War II, the lefty from Cincinnati joined the hundreds of women who were invited to Chicago's Wrigley Field in 1943 to try out for the AAGPBL's four original teams.

She made the Rockford (Illinois) Peaches and won the league batting title in 1946 and 1947. She also led the Peaches to the championship four times and made the All-Star team in seven of her 10 seasons.

In 1950, the Fort Lauderdale club of the Class B Florida International League, a men's minor league, tried to buy her contract, but the board of directors for the AAGPBL rejected the offer, saying, "Rockford couldn't afford to lose her."

In the 1992 movie *A League of Their Own*, the character Dottie Henson, portrayed as the star of the AAGPBL, was partially based on Kamenshek.

Atlanta 1996   PORTaPIT

Which sprinter was a 10-time U.S. 100-meter hurdle champion?

In the 1990s, **Gail Devers** traded U.S. and world records in the 100-meter hurdles with fellow UCLA star Jackie Joyner-Kersee, her training partner under Joyner-Kersee's husband, Bob Kersee, the Bruins' head coach. Devers was a three-time world champion in the event. However, she made her Olympic impact in a different dash, the 100-meter sprint (without hurdles). She won the race in 1992 and defended her title as the fastest woman in the world at the 1996 Games, where she also won gold in the 4 × 100 relay.

At the prestigious Millrose Games in New York City in 2007, a 40-year-old Devers won the 60-meter indoor hurdles, the event in which she had been a world champion in 2003. "People thought I went away," she said after the Millrose Games. "I always knew I could come back."

Who was the first player to dunk in a WNBA game?

Running down the court on a breakaway in a 2002 game against the Miami Sol, **Lisa Leslie** corralled a pass from L.A. Sparks teammate Latasha Byears. Leslie dribbled once; she dribbled twice. She took two steps with the ball and floated to the basket. Then: *Slam!* She dunked the ball, becoming the first woman to do so in a WNBA game. Later that summer, she led the Sparks to their second title and earned her second Finals MVP award.

Leslie, who was a four-time All-America at USC, led Team USA to four straight Olympic gold medals, beginning in 1996. She briefly retired after her first Games to pursue a career in modeling, but one year afterward, she was back on the court to play in the inaugural season of the WNBA. "I thought it was a summer league," she said upon her retirement—12 years later! A three-time league MVP and eight-time member of the All-WNBA first-team, Leslie was the league's most famous player and a gracious ambassador for the sport. She joined fellow USC Trojan Cheryl Miller in the basketball Hall of Fame in 2015.

DID YOU KNOW?

In 1984, Georgeann Wells of West Virginia slammed home the first dunk in a college game. Two years later, Leslie entered Morningside High in Inglewood, California. As a ninth grader, Leslie was a little over 6'2", and she dunked frequently throughout high school, where she was class president three out of four years.

FAST FACT: *When Leslie was a senior at Morningside, she scored 101 points in the first half of a game against South Torrance High. She didn't get the chance to add to her total, though: South Torrance forfeited at halftime.*

Which U.S. player kicked the game-winning penalty shot to win the 1999 World Cup?

After one period of overtime, the U.S. and China were still tied at zero in the 1999 World Cup final. It was time for penalty kicks. "Do you think you can make it?" an assistant coach on Team USA asked **Brandi Chastain.**

"Yeah, I do," replied Chastain. Ten minutes later, she did, breaking the 4–4 tie in penalty kicks. She booted the ball with her left foot because she had been struggling when using her right. "I told myself, Don't look at the goalkeeper," she said later. "It's probably a good thing I didn't think about the kick itself."

One of the best attacking defenders in the world, Chastain was on the squads that won Olympic gold in 1996 and 2004 and silver in 2000.

DID YOU KNOW?

China had already missed a penalty kick, so the game ended on Chastain's shot. She took off her jersey to celebrate, as many male soccer players had done before her. Because she was a woman, her decision made news. (She was wearing a Nike sports bra; the company was ecstatic.) She was on magazine covers and landed a coveted spot on Wheaties cereal boxes. Her iconic pose became a symbol of empowerment for girls everywhere.

Which LPGA tour golfer has the most single-season wins?

I n 1964, SPORTS ILLUSTRATED called her "the best woman golfer of all time," and **Mickey Wright** was only 29 years old. "She is such a long hitter, so accurate, and so dedicated to the game, that many observers are surprised she does not win every tournament she enters."

True, but she sure did win a lot. One year earlier, she had set the record for single-season victories on the LPGA tour (13), and in 1964, she won 11 tournaments, now tied with Annika Sorenstam for the second-best season of all time.

Though she retired when she was 34—Wright did not enjoy being in the spotlight—she is second on the LPGA tour's all-time wins list (82). She is also second in major tournament wins (13) and ended her career with records for lowest round (62) and most birdies in a round (nine).

FAST FACT:
Wright was 17 when she won her first national title, the 1952 USGA Girls' Junior championship.

Which tennis player received the Presidential Medal of Freedom?

It's the highest honor a civilian can receive in the United States, and in 2009, Barack Obama bestowed the Presidential Medal of Freedom on **Billie Jean King** for her accomplishments on and off the tennis court. King won a record 20 championships at Wimbledon (in singles, doubles, and mixed doubles, now tied with Martina Navratilova for most in history) and was the first woman to earn Sports Illustrated Sportsperson of the Year honors (in 1972). King was also a champion of equality as a player, president of the Women's Tennis Association, and founder of the Women's Sports Foundation. In 2006, the tennis complex in Queens, New York, that hosts the U.S. Open was renamed in King's honor.

DID YOU KNOW?

More than 30,000 people showed up at the Astrodome in Houston, Texas, in 1973 to see King play Bobby Riggs *(far right)* in a much-hyped match that became known as the Battle of the Sexes. She won in straight sets, took home $100,000 in prize money, and scored a victory for the women's movement. In 2017, the story of that match became a movie starring Emma Stone as King.

> **"** *[Sport] teaches us about daily living. Certain things don't always go our way. Sometimes we have to lose and we all must face it. Ups and downs. Hills and valleys. That's what sport is all about.* **That's what life is about, too**.*"*
>
> —*in 1972, upon being named* SPORTS ILLUSTRATED *Sportsperson of the Year alongside UCLA coach John Wooden*

3.

These stars broke down barriers and set sports on a new path

BLAZERS

Who was the first girl to pitch a shutout in the Little League World Series?

The summer before she started eighth grade was a momentous one for **Mo'ne Davis.** After throwing a complete-game, two-hit shutout against an all-boys' team from Tennessee in the 2014 Little League World Series, she became an overnight sensation, receiving messages on social media from First Lady Michelle Obama, NBA superstar Kevin Durant, and many others. She struck out eight and did not walk a single batter in a 4–0 victory for her All-Star team from Philadelphia. "It was nerve-racking, but I kept cool," she said. "My team told me, 'Go out and do what you do and we'll back you up.' They did. But me getting a shutout? I was a little shocked. I did it before, but this was a bigger stage."

A talented soccer athlete who wants to play basketball in college, Mo'ne was the first Little Leaguer to appear on the cover of SPORTS ILLUSTRATED.

DID YOU KNOW?

Mo'ne, the 18th girl to play in the LLWS, was on the cover of the August 25, 2014, edition of SPORTS ILLUSTRATED and also graced the front of the December issue of SI KIDS, having been named the SportsKid of the Year. "I just thought I was going to play baseball in the summer, have fun with my friends, then go back to school this fall," she told SI during the LLWS. "But now, because everything got so big and because we're doing well, I do feel like a role model."

WOW FACTOR

14

Batters Davis struck out in two starts in the 2014 LLWS. She only allowed one walk in 8⅓ innings.

Who founded the Special Olympics?

In 1962, **Eunice Kennedy Shriver** held a summer camp for young people with intellectual disabilities at her home outside Washington, D.C. Fifty-three years later, the 2015 Special Olympics World Summer Games drew more than 7,000 athletes from 177 countries, 40,000 volunteers, and 500,000 spectators. Shriver was a visionary who focused on inclusion, and who wanted to give a voice to people with disabilities who had been ignored, such as her sister Rosemary.

Today, the Special Olympics movement includes 4.9 million athletes—competitors range from eight years old to adults—who participate in programs in 172 countries.

Said Shriver at the 1991 World Summer Games opening ceremony, "Come to our world, where we speak from our souls as we demand equality from our legislators and our educators, for we are the peacemakers."

> " *You are the stars, and the world is watching you. By your presence, you send a message to every village, every city, every nation— a message of hope, a **message of victory**.* "
>
> *—in 1987, to athletes at the opening ceremony of the Special Olympics World Summer Games in South Bend, Indiana*

Who was the first female athlete to play in the NHL?

During a Tampa Bay Lightning preseason game in 1992, 20-year-old **Manon Rheaume** became the first woman to play in an NHL game, stopping seven of the nine shots that came her way. She only appeared in one other exhibition, but she went on to play five seasons in the minors. "At the time I didn't realize what I was doing," she said a decade later. "I look at the game, how fast it is, how hard the guys shoot, and I can't believe I was there." The native of Quebec won world championships with Canada's women's team in 1992 and 1994, and helped the squad take silver at the 1998 Olympics.

FAST FACT:
Clark, who has won more than 70 events in her career, had a breakout moment when she won the U.S. Snowboard Grand Prix title as a 17-year-old.

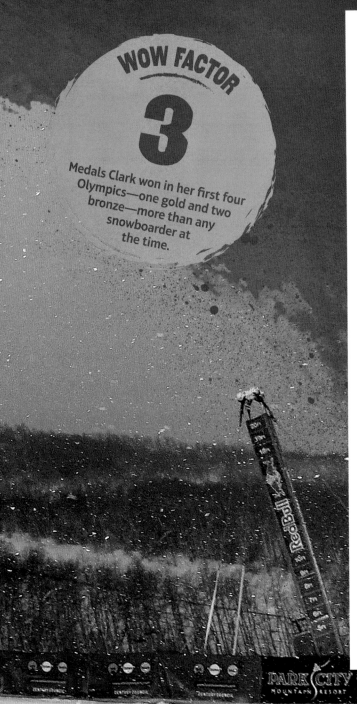

WOW FACTOR

3

Medals Clark won in her first four Olympics—one gold and two bronze—more than any snowboarder at the time.

Which snowboarder has more halfpipe medals than any woman in X Games history?

Through the end of 2017 she had 14 X Games medals, seven of them gold, but **Kelly Clark** has done more than win hardware during her celebrated snowboarding career. She has changed the way athletes compete. She was the first woman to land a 1080—a move that requires three full rotations in midair—in halfpipe competition.

Clark, who attended Mount Snow Academy while growing up in Vermont, was racing on skis as a first-grader. By the time she was 11, however, she had made her preference known: She would much rather be snowboarding than skiing.

She was 19 when she won her first Olympic medal, a gold in 2002, just four years after the sport made its debut at the Games.

Which skateboarder was the first woman to turn pro?

This photo of **Patti McGee** appeared on the cover of LIFE magazine in May 1965, the year after the San Diego native won the national girls' championship and shortly after she became the first woman to turn pro in the sport. "It's still changing my life," she said in 2017. "I get requests for autographs all the time." At 19 years old she was in commercials (skateboarding through the house to answer the phone) and on talk shows, showing off this fancy move and others while serving as a spokesperson for Hobie skateboards.

McGee started out as a surfer, having taken up the hobby when she was 13. "Skateboarding was something to do in the afternoon when the surf was blown out," she said.

Her sport has certainly become flashier over the last six decades, but McGee was a true pioneer. She was inducted into the Skateboarding Hall of Fame in 2010.

FAST FACT:
When McGee was 16, her brother fashioned their first skateboard from her roller skate wheels and a plank he cut at wood shop.

Who was the first woman to play in a men's pro basketball league?

Known for her physical style on the court, point guard **Nancy Lieberman** was the preeminent player of her day. She became the youngest basketball player to ever win an Olympic medal when she helped Team USA earn silver in 1976 as a 17-year-old. She then led Old Dominion to consecutive national titles (1979, 1980) and a 72–2 record as a junior and senior.

Her career was far from over after her run of dominance at ODU. She played in the New York Pro Summer League alongside men after graduation to stay in shape, then played for the Dallas Diamonds in two different women's pro leagues. In 1986, the men's United States Basketball League called, and Lieberman played for the Springfield Fame that year and the Long Island Knights in 1987. She went on to become a head coach in the WNBA with the Detroit Shock and an assistant in the NBA with the Sacramento Kings.

Said Lieberman upon being inducted into the Hall of Fame in 1996, "Basketball has given me . . . my confidence, my self-esteem, the ability to share with teammates, to be responsible, to learn how to win, and also to learn how to lose."

WOW FACTOR

7

Days Lieberman signed to play for the Detroit Shock of the WNBA in 2008, when she was 50 years old.

Which sprinter overcame paralysis to win three Olympic gold medals?

When she was four years old, **Wilma Rudolph,** the 20th of 22 children growing up in a poor household in Tennessee, had double pneumonia and scarlet fever at the same time. She was so sick that she almost died, and her left leg was paralyzed. It wasn't until she was eight years old that she began to walk, using a leg brace. Three years later she was able to play basketball, and by the time she was 16, she was on the U.S. Olympic track and field team. She helped the 4 × 100-meter relay team win bronze at the 1956 Games.

When she returned to the Olympics in 1960, she became a superstar. She won the 100, the 200, and anchored the winning 4 × 100 relay team to gold. "I just run," she said afterward. "I don't know why I run so fast."

FAST FACT:
Rudolph was one of the famed Tennessee State Tigerbelles who combined to win 13 Olympic gold medals under coach Ed Temple.

Which tennis player won 90 of 92 matches at Wimbledon?

Not only was she near perfect at Wimbledon in singles, doubles, and mixed doubles, but **Suzanne Lenglen** also won six of the seven singles *and* doubles titles at the French Championships held between 1920 and 1926.

The native of France was a genuine superstar, a celebrity who pushed the boundaries of what was acceptable for women at the time. She wore nail polish *(gasp!)*, red lipstick, and short-sleeved dresses with hems that hit above her calves.

When she was 14, she won the 1914 world hard-court championships in Paris, but World War I interrupted her career. After the war, she lost only one singles match in eight years and was ranked number one in the world from 1921 through 1926.

Which surfer founded the first women's pro tour?

When she began surfing competitively at the age of 16, **Rell Sunn** entered men's events because there were none for women. Within a decade, she had helped found the first professional tour for women, in 1975. By 1982, she was the top-ranked pro woman in the world. One year later, at 32, she was diagnosed with breast cancer. Throughout her treatment, she was an advocate for creating educational programs about the disease for women in her home state of Hawaii and organized an annual surf contest for kids. She died after a 14-year battle with cancer.

FAST FACT:
Sunn and the other women on the pro tour founded Women's Professional Surfing in 1979 to bring up issues such as pay inequality that they faced in their sport.

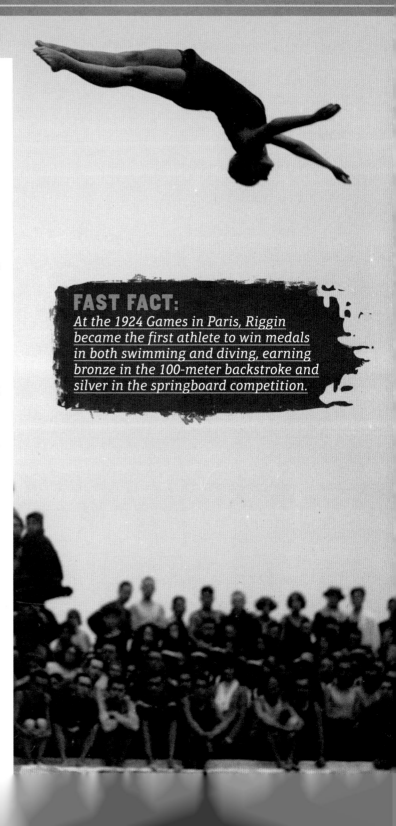

Which American diver became an Olympic gold medalist at 14 years old?

The United States Olympic Committee reluctantly allowed 14-year-old **Aileen Riggin** and two other girls her age to compete at the 1920 Games, having been assured the athletes would not let the U.S. down. So Riggin, all 65 pounds of her, and her compatriots boarded the Princess Matoika, a troop transport ship that had survived World War I. It was loaded with supplies for Allied forces overseas, plus the 400 members of the Olympic team. "Our hearts sank a little when we saw the old tub," Riggin said years afterward, "but we really didn't care. We were all excited to finally be going."

Thirteen days later, they arrived in Antwerp, Belgium, where it was cold, windy, and overcast. The water was so dark during practice, Riggin couldn't tell which way was up once she landed her dives. "On several occasions I became frightened when I felt I was lost and running out of air," she recalled.

On the day of the springboard competition, she went last and executed her final dive with a clean entry, something the other divers had not done. The judges took several hours to tally the scores, but sure enough: Riggin had won!

FAST FACT:
At the 1924 Games in Paris, Riggin became the first athlete to win medals in both swimming and diving, earning bronze in the 100-meter backstroke and silver in the springboard competition.

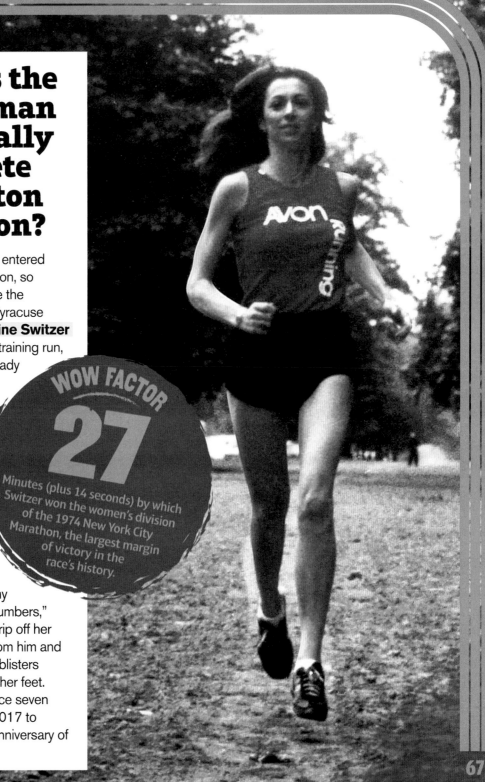

Who was the first woman to officially complete the Boston Marathon?

No woman had ever entered the Boston Marathon, so three weeks before the 1967 race, 19-year-old Syracuse University student **Kathrine Switzer** completed 31 miles on a training run, just to be sure she was ready to tackle the 26.2-mile race. The next day, she signed up for Boston as K.V. Switzer.

On a snowy Patriots' Day, April 19, Switzer, her boyfriend, and her coach lined up at the start, and they were off! Four miles into the race, an official spotted her. "Get out of my race and give me those numbers," he shouted as he tried to rip off her race bib. She got away from him and ran all 26.2 miles despite blisters popping on the arches of her feet. She went on to run the race seven more times, including in 2017 to commemorate the 50th anniversary of her accomplishment.

WOW FACTOR

27

Minutes (plus 14 seconds) by which Switzer won the women's division of the 1974 New York City Marathon, the largest margin of victory in the race's history.

Who was the first African-American tennis player to compete in the U.S. National Championships?

When she won the 1957 U.S. Open, **Althea Gibson** received the trophy from Vice President Richard Nixon. "I hope to wear my crown with dignity and humility," she said. Gibson indeed displayed great dignity and humility throughout a brief but phenomenal tennis career during which she won 56 tournaments, five singles Grand Slams, and five doubles Grand Slams in eight years.

In 1950, she had become the first African-American to play in the U.S. National Championships, which was later renamed the U.S. Open. She didn't win her first major, the French Championships (now the French Open), until 1956. The following year she won the other three: the Australian Championships (now the Australian Open), Wimbledon, and the U.S. Open. She won the latter two tournaments again in 1958. Before her 1957 U.S. Open victory, she appeared on the cover of SPORTS ILLUSTRATED. "Her forceful game has reached the point," the story said, "where she seems to win almost without trying."

Gibson was far from finished with professional sports when her tennis career ended: She went on to become the first African-American golfer to join the LPGA tour.

SPORTS ILLUSTRATED

ALTHEA GIBSON MEETS HER BIGGEST TEST AT FOREST HILLS

WOW FACTOR

171

Golf tournaments Gibson played on the LPGA tour from 1963 through 1977.

DID YOU **KNOW?**

After Gibson won Wimbledon in 1957, she returned to her hometown of New York City, where she was honored with a ticker-tape parade downtown that ended in front of City Hall. Mayor Robert F. Wagner Jr. told the crowd he was proud that she was "a New York girl who learned the game here." He added, "If we had more wonderful people like you, the world would be a better place."

Who was the first woman to reach the summit of Mount Everest?

n May 1975, 35-year-old Japanese mountaineer **Junko Tabei** led 14 women on an ascent of the 29,029-foot peak. Two-thirds of the way up Everest, while the group slept, an avalanche buried the climbers. They survived thanks to the six Sherpas, or guides, on their expedition, who pulled them out of the snow. Tabei was unable to walk at first but was determined to continue. She resumed the ascent two days later and became the first woman, and 36th person, to summit the world's tallest mountain.

In addition to becoming the first woman to climb the highest peaks on each continent, a feat she accomplished in 1992, Tabei was an environmentalist and preservationist. She opened the door for female climbers everywhere but especially in Japan, where women were discouraged from being adventurous.

She earned fame but shied away from the perks that came with it. "Climbing the mountain," she said, "is its own reward."

Who led her AAU team to wins in 91 of 92 games?

A singular talent during basketball's early days, **Nera White** went to Peabody College, which did not have a team. Nearby Nashville Business College sponsored an AAU team, though, and White joined. She proceeded to lead that squad to 10 AAU national titles, including eight in a row from 1962 through 1969. Plus, she was a 15-time AAU All-America and a 10-time MVP of the AAU tournament.

White was also an elite softball player: She was All-World in 1959 and 1965 for the Amateur Softball Association fast-pitch team.

In 1992, White and Lusia Harris-Stewart were the first two women inducted into the basketball Hall of Fame.

Which polo star played matches dressed like a man?

Known as A. Jones on the playing field, **Sue Sally Hale** used mascara to draw a fake moustache and played polo with the guys in the 1950s and 1960s. "I pushed my long hair under a hat and wore a large shirt," she said later. "I never spoke a word. Only the guys on my team knew I was a girl."

In 1972, the U.S. Polo Association finally admitted women, in part because of pressure from Hale and her friends.

As a 53-year-old grandmother, she and her daughters Sunny and Stormie were on a team that won the inaugural USPA Women's Open Tournament Championship.

Who was the first NCAA coach to reach 1,000 victories?

DID YOU KNOW?

Pat Head (Summitt was her married name) played basketball at Tennessee-Martin and on the U.S. Olympic team that won silver at the 1976 Games (two years after she took the Tennessee job). She went on to coach Team USA to gold at the 1984 Olympics.

When **Pat Summitt** arrived at the University of Tennessee to coach basketball in 1974, she drove the team van. Women's basketball finally became an NCAA championship sport in 1981–1982, and Summitt's Lady Vols were considered *the* elite program for two decades, winning eight national championships between 1987 and 2008 and appearing in five other title games.

The court at the basketball arena was named the Summitt in 2005. One year later, she became the first women's basketball coach to earn $1 million a year. Summitt retired in 2012 with more wins (1,098) than anyone in women's or men's college basketball history. She suffered from Alzheimer's and in the last years of her life worked to raise awareness about the disease.

Who was the first high school basketball player to make the women's national team?

While at Sonora High in Southern California, point guard **Ann Meyers Drysdale** was already on the national team! She became the first woman to receive a full athletic scholarship to UCLA, then helped Team USA win silver in 1976, the year women's basketball made its Olympic debut. She was a four-time All-America for the Bruins, and in 2017, the practice court at the school's women's basketball facility was named after her.

The Indiana Pacers made her the first woman signed to an NBA contract in 1979, though they cut her in a preseason camp.

FAST FACT:
Against Stephen F. Austin State University in 1978, Meyers Drysdale had the first ever quadruple double in Division I history (20 points, 14 rebounds, 10 assists, and 10 steals).

Who is the most famous roller derby athlete of all time?

Roller derby is not a sport for the faint of heart. **Ann Calvello** embraced aggressiveness on the track while being an ambassador for the sport off it. She had personality—and plenty of it. She dyed her hair all sorts of crazy colors and also with patterns, such as polka dots and stars. When she died in 2006, SPORTS ILLUSTRATED remembered her as "simply, the best villain there ever was in sport. She was the Meanest Mama on Skates and the Queen of the Penalty Box—and proud of it. She was also a terrific athlete."

Which track and field athlete won four gold medals at the 1948 Olympics?

The Olympics were old hat for **Fanny Blankers-Koen** by the time the 1948 Games in London rolled around. She had tied for sixth in the high jump in Berlin in 1936, but World War II delayed her track and field career. She was 30 years old, with two children, when she arrived at the 1948 Olympics from the Netherlands holding world records in the high jump and the long jump. And she didn't even enter those events! She ran the 100- and 200-meter races and the 80-meter hurdles—and won them all. She also anchored the 4 × 100 relay team to gold, despite being about five meters behind when she took the baton.

FAST FACT:
Blankers-Koen, who was nicknamed the Flying Housewife, had a candy bar named after her following the 1948 Olympics.

Who was the first woman to win Triple Crown and Breeders' Cup races?

Growing up in Michigan, **Julie Krone** learned to ride before she learned to walk. She got her start as a groom and an exercise rider at famed Churchill Downs in Kentucky before she was 16. At 17, she won her first race, at Tampa Bay Downs in 1980. Through the early days of her career, she encountered many obstacles: trainers and owners who didn't want to hire her, fellow jockeys who didn't want to ride with her, and plenty of fans who didn't think women should be jockeys.

But she was good, and before she had turned 25, she had 1,200 wins. She was the first woman to win a riding title at a major track (in 1987 at New Jersey racecourses Monmouth Park, the Meadowlands, and Atlantic City); the first to win a Triple Crown race (the 1993 Belmont Stakes astride Colonial Affair); and the first to win a Breeders' Cup race (in 2003 aboard Halfbridled).

In 2000, Krone became the first woman inducted into the National Museum of Racing's Hall of Fame.

WOW FACTOR

3,704

Victories Krone had when she retired in 2004. She was the first woman to surpass 3,500 wins.

Who was the first woman to swim the English Channel?

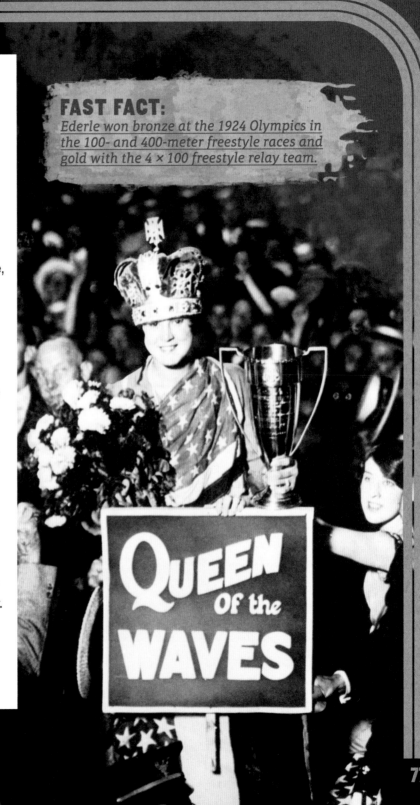

The final three hours of her 14-hour, 31-minute swim from Cape Gris-Nez, France, across the English Channel were brutal for **Gertrude Ederle.** The current pushed against her, and rain pounded the choppy water that August day in 1926 as she tried to become the first woman to complete the swim. She had been disqualified during the 23rd mile of her attempt in 1925, after one of her support-team members touched her. (Her team thought she was drowning; she was just resting.)

In 1926, she fought against the current until it turned in her favor, and when she waded ashore in Kingsdown, England, Ederle had finished the swim two hours faster than any of the five men before her. She returned to the States, where an estimated two million people showed up in New York City for a ticker-tape parade in her honor.

QUEEN OF the WAVES

RECOR

4.

These women set new standards for excellence

D BREAKERS

" *I'm really proud of the player I was, and I will be proud of the **athletes who break my records**."*

—in 2017, at the College at Brockport

Who has scored more goals than anyone in international soccer history?

No soccer player has been better at heading the ball into the net than **Abby Wambach,** so it was not surprising that one of the four goals she scored for the U.S. women's national team in a 5–0 win over South Korea in 2013 was a header. Oh, and that header, her 159th goal, made Wambach the game's all-time leading scorer among women and men. "It's just a mathematical equation," the 5'11" Wambach said of how she became so successful at knocking the ball with her noggin. "I'm taller. I can jump. And when you're shooting with your head, it's impossible for goalkeepers to know where the ball is going." She retired in 2015 with 184 goals, two Olympic gold medals, and a record six U.S. Soccer Female Athlete of the Year awards.

She capped off her career by helping Team USA win the World Cup, the major honor that had eluded her.

FAST FACT:
Wambach, the 2012 FIFA Player of the Year, is one of only two Americans to have earned the award. (Mia Hamm won in 2001 and 2002.)

Who owns the WNBA career scoring record?

In 2017, when she became the leading scorer in WNBA history (7,489 points), **Diana Taurasi** merely gave basketball fans another reason to consider her one of the greatest players of all time.

It would have been devastating for the game (though much better for her opponents) if Taurasi had stuck with her plan to quit the game in favor of soccer when she was 11. Her hiatus from the hard court only lasted for a year, though.

At 18, the nation's top recruit began her career at Connecticut, then led the Huskies to three straight NCAA titles. Shortly after graduation, she helped Team USA win Olympic gold. Taurasi was just getting warmed up: She went on to win three more gold medals, three WNBA titles with the Phoenix Mercury, and five WNBA scoring titles.

WOW FACTOR

6

EuroLeague championships Taurasi has won while playing overseas in the WNBA offseason, a record.

FAST FACT:
McCormick's daughter, Kelly, won springboard silver at the 1984 Olympics and bronze at the 1988 Games.

Who is the only female diver to have won back-to-back Olympic golds in springboard and platform?

She was the kind of kid who would do a cannonball off a bridge near her home in California just as a boat was passing underneath to try to splash the passengers. The idea of swimming laps bored **Pat McCormick,** also known as Patsy Pest. But diving? That was fun. Her combination of coordination and timing, along with her eagerness to compete, gave her an instant edge. She began training with the Los Angeles Athletic Club at 16 and only missed the 1948 Olympic team as an 18-year-old by .01 of a point.

McCormick stuck with the sport, sweeping the five U.S. titles in 1951 and going on to win gold in the three-meter springboard and the 10-meter platform at the 1952 Olympics. Her hometown of Long Beach welcomed her home with a parade!

In 1956, less than a year after giving birth to her son, Tim, she was favored to repeat as double champion at that year's Summer Games. After all, she had won 27 national titles by that point. She didn't disappoint, once again taking home two golds and earning Associated Press Female Athlete of the Year.

Who is the only American woman to win six medals in one Olympics?

When she was 10 months old, **Natalie Coughlin** got her start in a pool in her backyard in California. At six, she was competing, and by 16, she had set multiple national age-group records. Slowed by a shoulder injury that year, she narrowly missed the 2000 Olympics. "It was frustrating and depressing," she said, "especially because my earlier times would have made the team." How did Coughlin react? At the 2004 Games, she went out and won five medals: gold in the 100-meter backstroke and with the 4 × 200-meter freestyle relay team; two relay silvers; and bronze in the 100-meter free. She outdid herself in 2008, winning six medals—including a repeat gold in the 100 backstroke—to set the record.

Who is the only runner to simultaneously hold U.S. records at every distance from 800 to 10,000 meters?

In 1974, a pigtailed 15-year-old named **Mary Decker** set world indoor records at 800 meters, and at 880 and 1,000 yards. In 1983, when she was named SPORTS ILLUSTRATED's Sportsperson of the Year, she won the 1,500 and 3,000 meters at the world championships, held seven U.S. records, and had set seven world records in the previous two years. She famously fell in the 3,000 final at the 1984 Olympics but set two world records the following year.

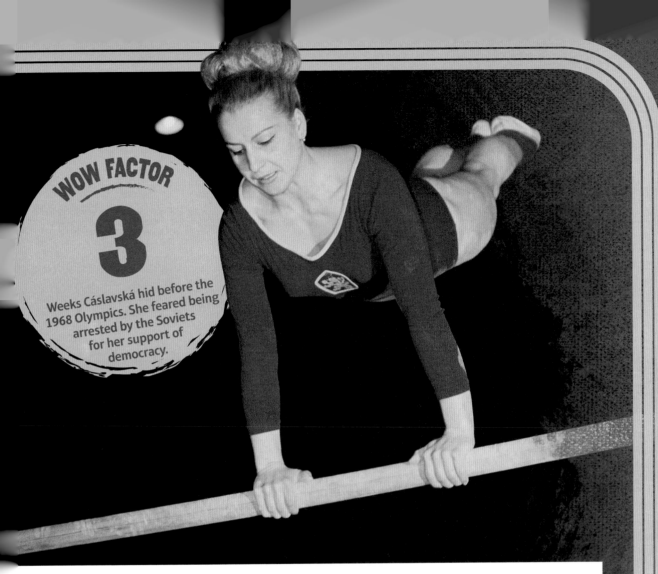

Who is the only female gymnast to have won Olympic gold on every apparatus?

Throughout a sparkling career in the 1960s, **Vera Cáslavská** of Czechoslovakia (now part of the Czech Republic) was nothing if not versatile. At the 1964 Olympics, she won gold in the vault and all-around and on the balance beam, and helped her country win silver in the team event.

During the 1968 Games, the fan favorite won gold in the vault, floor exercise, uneven bars, and all-around. She took silver on the balance beam and in the team event. She also became known for her willingness to take a stand against injustice. The Soviet Union had two months earlier invaded Czechoslovakia. Standing on the podium to be recognized for sharing gold in the floor exercise with Larisa Petrik of the Soviet Union, Cáslavská bowed her head and looked away from the flag as the Soviet anthem played.

Which swimmer holds the women's record for most world championships?

When **Katie Ledecky** won the 1,500 meters at the 2017 world championships by 19 seconds (yes, you read that correctly), she brought her career gold medal total at the event to 12, a record for female swimmers. By the end of the competition, she had 14. She has simply dominated freestyle events, winning in the 200-, 400-, 800-, and 1,500-meter races, and in both relays.

Ledecky was only 15 and the youngest member of Team USA when she won the 800 at the 2012 Olympics. At the 2016 Games, where she was again the youngest U.S. swimmer, she became the first athlete to sweep the 200, 400, and 800 meters in nearly 50 years, and she earned gold and silver in two relays. That fall, she began her freshman year at Stanford and proceeded to help the Cardinal win their first NCAA title since 1998.

By the time the 2016 Olympics were over, Ledecky was considered one of the greatest swimmers of all time. She set a world record in the 400 freestyle and lowered her own world record in the 800 by nearly two seconds. In the latter race, her last of the Games, she won by 11 seconds. "She could still be swimming in 2024," Hall of Famer Janet Evans said that summer. "She's so far ahead, stratospherically ahead, that [if] she wants to, she could swim for a very long time."

FAST FACT:
At Stanford, Ledecky became the second freshman to ever win the Honda Cup Award, given to the nation's most outstanding female collegiate athlete.

Who was the first athlete to win medals at six straight Summer Olympics?

Immediately after winning gold in skeet shooting at the 2012 Olympics to become the first American to earn a medal at five consecutive Games, **Kim Rhode** of California was already looking ahead. "The oldest medalist in the history of the Olympics was a shooter who was 72," she said, referring to Oscar Swahn of Sweden, who won silver in 1920. "So I have a few in me."

Four years later, at 37, she took bronze in skeet to extend her streak to six Games, the longest for a female athlete. (Luger Armin Zoeggeler of Italy medaled in six straight Winter Olympics, from 1994 to 2014.)

Rhode's Olympic journey began when she won gold in double trap as a rising high school senior at the 1996 Games. She won bronze in 2000 and gold again in 2004, after which the event was eliminated in favor of skeet shooting. (In double trap, two targets travel away from the athlete; in skeet, they move at an angle in front of the athlete.) She took silver in skeet in 2008, then gold and bronze. Don't be surprised if you see Rhode in Tokyo in 2020 and even in Los Angeles in 2024.

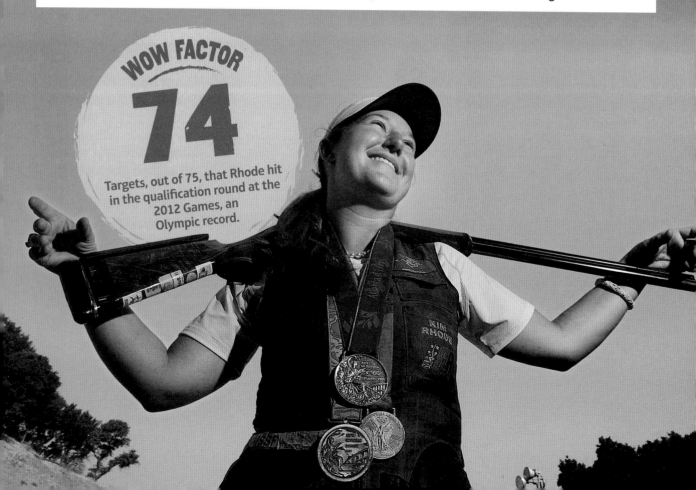

WOW FACTOR

74

Targets, out of 75, that Rhode hit in the qualification round at the 2012 Games, an Olympic record.

Which sailor made the quickest trip around the world?

It may sound like a really *(really)* long time, but it took 24-year-old **Ellen MacArthur** of England *only* 71 days, 14 hours, 18 minutes, and 33 seconds to sail around the world in 2005, the fastest time in history by 32 hours. She traveled 27,354 miles during that time, averaging four hours of sleep a day—20 minutes here, 20 minutes there.

MacArthur took her first ride on a sailboat when she was four, and she was hooked. On her first day of a weeklong sailing course in grade school, she capsized 11 times and was last or next-to-last in each race. "On my way home I promised myself never to be last again," she said in 2005. "No matter what it took."

Who was the first athlete to win four Final Four Most Outstanding Player awards?

Already recognized as the nation's top player entering her freshman year at the University of Connecticut in 2012, **Breanna Stewart** was expected to do great things during her college career. No one could have anticipated just how great those things would be—except possibly Stewart herself.

After leading the Huskies to four straight NCAA titles and becoming the only women's or men's player to earn four Final Four MOP awards, she said, "I had the perfect ending to a college career. My goal coming in as a freshman at UConn was to win four national championships." Mission accomplished!

WOW FACTOR

414

Shots Stewart blocked
while at UConn, a program
career record.

FAST FACT:
*The Seattle Storm selected Stewart
first in the 2016 WNBA draft, and she
went on to win league rookie of the
year that season.*

178

Goals Granato scored for Concordia University in Montreal while earning a master's degree in sports administration.

Who is the all-time leading scorer in women's international hockey?

Growing up in a hockey-crazed family in Illinois, **Cammi Granato** played for a boys' team until she was 16, around the time her older brother Tony began his 13-year NHL career. She became a superstar for Providence College and was a founding member of the U.S. women's national team, which took silver at the first-ever women's world championships, in 1990.

Eight years later, at the first Olympics in which women's hockey was included as a sport, Granato was the captain of the U.S. team that upset Canada to win gold.

She was instrumental in helping women's hockey find its footing in the U.S. Granato retired in 2005 with a record 54 international goals. In 2010 she was the first woman inducted into the Hockey Hall of Fame.

Which softball pitcher holds the record for most perfect games in NCAA Division I history?

Reporters called her "the most spellbinding pitcher in college softball" and "the best curveball pitcher in the world." In her four seasons at the University of Texas, **Cat Osterman** threw a record nine perfect games and was named national player of the year three times. While with the Longhorns, Osterman helped Team USA win gold at the 2004 Olympics. The lefty also led the squad to silver at the 2008 Games.

Osterman went on to play eight seasons in the National Pro Fastpitch league, earning three pitcher of the year awards, six All-NPF nods, and four championships.

FAST FACT:

In her nine years playing for USA Softball, Osterman was 59–4 with a stunning 0.38 earned run average.

Which tennis player had the longest streak of consecutive years with a Grand Slam victory?

Serena Williams has claimed most of the major women's tennis records, but **Chris Evert** was the darling of American tennis two decades before her, dominating the WTA Tour and winning at least one Grand Slam tournament in each season from 1974 through 1986. During those 13 years, she racked up victories at the Australian Open (two), the French Open (seven), Wimbledon (three), and the U.S. Open (six).

Evert was the first woman to hit the $1 million mark in earnings on the court and was named the Associated Press Female Athlete of the Year four times. She had an intense rivalry with Martina Navratilova, whom Evert faced in 14 Grand Slam finals, winning four.

WOW FACTOR

125

Consecutive matches Evert won on clay courts, a record among women and men for any surface.

FAST FACT:
Evert worked as a tennis analyst for NBC for 10 years and has been a broadcaster for ESPN since 2011.

DID YOU **KNOW?**

In December 1976, after winning 44 of the 62 tournaments she had entered over a three-year period, Evert was named SPORTS ILLUSTRATED's Sportsperson of the Year. "What makes her a champion who each year moves further and further beyond the reach of mortal tennis players, is grit," the story read. "Chris Evert has true grit. Character. Mental tenacity. She is a clear thinker in a thoughtful game. And she never gives up."

Who has the most pro golf victories?

During each year that passed in the 1960s and 1970s, **Kathy Whitworth** just kept winning. Eight victories here (1963), another seven there (1965). A whopping 10 (1968)! And seven more (1973)!

Then in July 1984, in a sudden-death playoff against Rosie Jones at the Rochester International golf tournament in New York, Whitworth bagged her 85th victory to become the winningest professional golfer in history. Sam Snead, the PGA Tour icon, had previously held the record. "Sam was just great about it," Whitworth, who retired with 88 wins, said years later. "He called me in the press room when it finally happened."

Tiger Woods, who through the end of 2017 had 79 wins on the PGA Tour, is the only active golfer within 45 victories of Whitworth's record.

FAST FACT:

Twice named the Associated Press Female Athlete of the Year, Whitworth won the Vare Trophy, given to the LPGA tour member with the lowest scoring average, a record seven times.

Which swimmer's world records in the 100- and 200-meter butterfly stood for nearly two decades?

Because one of her 10 siblings was also named Mary, **Mary T. Meagher** went by Mary T (for Terstegge, her mother's maiden name) while growing up in Kentucky. At the 1979 Pan American Games, before she even turned 15, Meagher set her first world record, in the 200-meter butterfly. Her best time in the event (2:05.96) came in the summer of 1981. Susie O'Neill of Australia finally broke the record in 2000.

Three days after Meagher set that 200-meter record, she swam a time in the 100 butterfly (57.93) that would stand almost as long: American Jenny Thompson broke it in 1999.

At 14, when asked how she was so good at such a challenging stroke, Meagher answered, "It's not hard for me. I like it. I was always a butterflyer. It's a stroke where you can't really loaf, 'cause you'll sink if you do."

WOW FACTOR

3

Number of gold medals Meagher won at the 1984 Olympics, in the 100 and 200 fly and on the butterfly leg of the 4 × 100 medley relay.

Who is the only swimmer to set American records in all four strokes?

A s a 15-year-old with braces on her teeth, **Tracy Caulkins** broke five U.S. records at the 1978 AAU National Short Course Championships. Then she won five golds at the world championships that year. She was gearing up for the 1980 Olympics, but the U.S. boycotted the Games for political reasons. "I suppose I could be over the hill in 1984," she said that summer.

Far from it. When the U.S. Olympic Trials rolled around, the 21-year-old was a 48-time national champ. She made the team, then won the 200- and 400-meter individual medleys and took gold with the U.S. 4 × 100 medley relay team.

Who is the most decorated Winter Olympian of all time?

A t the 2018 Games, cross-country skier **Marit Bjørgen** of Norway won her 11th, 12th, 13th, and 14th Olympic medals to put her at the top of the list. She then won the 30-kilometer mass start to end the Games with 15 career medals, eight of them gold (tied for most by any Winter Olympian). That haul is pretty impressive on its own, but through 2017, she had 26 world championship medals as well. She also had 111 World Cup wins, more than twice as many as any other woman.

Bjørgen has excelled at a variety of distances, having competed in the 10K (6.2 miles), 15K, and 30K. She earned her first medal as a 21-year-old at the 2002 Olympics, when Norway's 4 × 5K relay team took silver.

Which woman has the most Olympic medals in history?

Growing up in Ukraine, **Larisa Latynina** began ballet lessons when she was 11. One year later, the studio closed, so she took up gymnastics. The woman who entered the sport by chance now has more Olympic medals (18) than anyone except U.S. swimmer Michael Phelps (28).

Competing for the Soviet Union during the 1956, 1960, and 1964 Games, Latynina led her squad to three straight team victories. She also won back-to-back golds in the all-around competition before coming in second to Vera Cáslavská in 1964. (Cáslavská is the only other woman to successfully defend her Olympic all-around title.)

WOW FACTOR

9

Olympic gold medals Latynina won, most for a woman and tied for second among all athletes after Phelps (23).

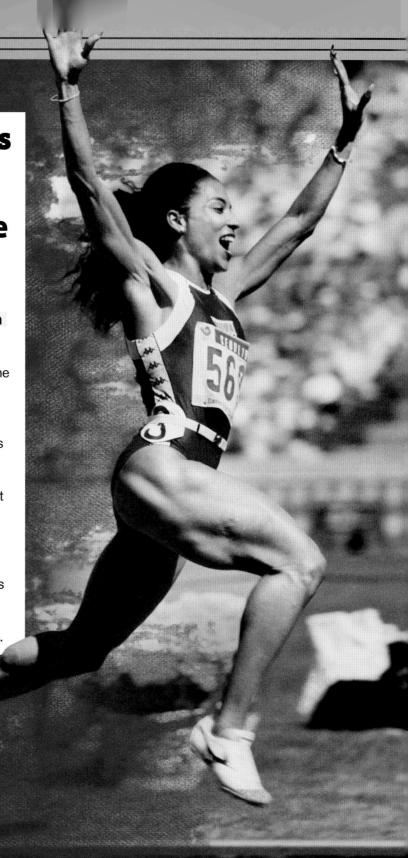

Which sprinter's world records in the 100 and 200 meters have stood since the 1980s?

K nown as Flo-Jo, **Florence Griffith Joyner** had flair—she sported colorful, long nails and one-legged unitards—and boy, was she fast. In fact, she became the fastest woman on the planet when she set a world record to win the 100-meter race at the 1988 U.S. Olympic Trials in Indianapolis (10.49). At the Games that summer, she won gold in the 100 and the 200, setting a world record in the latter (21.34). Both of those marks were still intact at the end of 2017. Her fashion sense brought her notoriety after her retirement in 1988: She was asked to design new uniforms for the NBA's Indiana Pacers. The team sported those duds for seven seasons in the 1990s. Griffith Joyner, who was married to track star Jackie Joyner-Kersee's brother, died at 38 after an epileptic seizure.

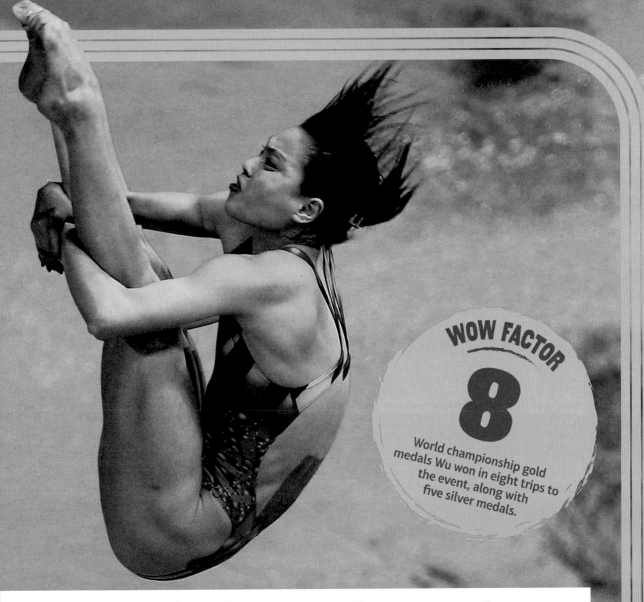

Who is the most decorated Olympic diver of all time?

At the 2016 Olympics, **Wu Minxia** did something no one had ever done before: She won a fourth gold medal in a single event, three-meter synchronized diving. The victory, with diving partner Shi Tingmao, brought Wu's career total to five gold medals and seven in all, giving her more golds and more hardware than any diver in history. (She took silver and bronze in the three-meter springboard event in 2004 and 2008, respectively, then won gold in 2012.)

Eighteen years old when she won her first gold, in 2004, at the 2016 Games, a 30-year-old Wu became the oldest female diver to win a gold medal. She retired from competition shortly afterward.

CH

AMPIONS

5.

*These winners
showed heart
and got results*

Who won four WNBA titles in her first seven seasons in the league?

When she was a freshman at UConn, forward **Maya Moore** was the top scorer for the Huskies and came in second in the Associated Press Player of the Year voting. After four years on campus, she had led the program to a 150–4 record and won two national championships (2009, 2010).

The Minnesota Lynx selected Moore with the first pick in the 2011 WNBA draft—and she just kept on winning. She earned Rookie of the Year while helping the Lynx to the championship that season, then led the team to titles in 2013, 2015, and 2017. And the honors have just kept rolling in: Moore was Finals MVP (2013), league MVP (2014), and was first-team All-WNBA from 2013 through 2017.

WOW FACTOR

149

Games Moore scored in double figures at UConn (out of 154 games played), an NCAA record.

"I love all my championships. I love to compete, and when you have the talent, the discipline, the work ethic, and teammates who do the same thing, **winning follows you around.**"

—in 2013, to SPORTS ILLUSTRATED

Who won more Olympic golds than any female swimmer in history?

Swimming is often thought of as an individual endeavor, but for American **Jenny Thompson,** the sport was very much about teamwork. Over four Olympics, she won a record eight gold medals, all in relays (three in the 4 × 100-meter freestyle, two in the 4 × 200, and three in the 4 × 100 medley). She also won two relay silvers, and silver and bronze in the 100 free in 1992 and 2000, respectively, bringing her total to 12 medals (tied with Americans Dara Torres and Natalie Coughlin for most by a female swimmer).

That's not to say that Thompson didn't have success on her own: In 1992, she became the first U.S. woman in 61 years to break the world record in the 100 free. And in 2004, she won the 50-meter butterfly at the world championships, then retired from swimming so she could complete her final two years at Columbia medical school.

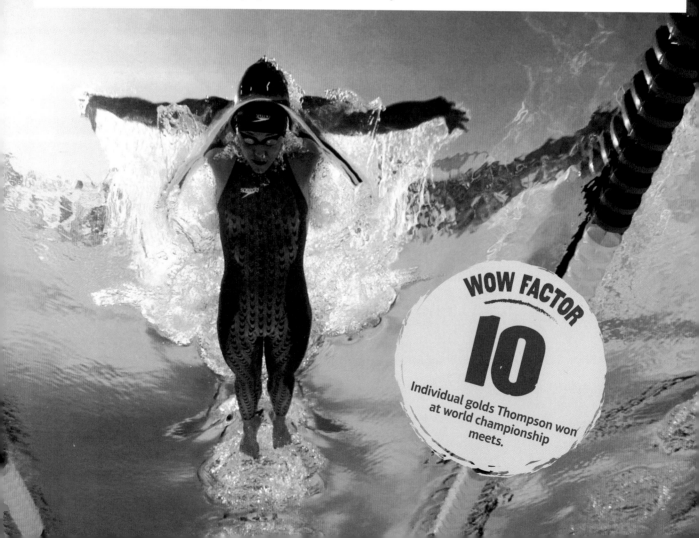

WOW FACTOR

10

Individual golds Thompson won at world championship meets.

> *It's taken a lot of hard work and dedication, trying to teach society what it means to be a Paralympian, that **we're not any different,** that we're just like the Olympians, with the same training sites, sponsorships, medals, and venues.*

—*in 2016, to* **The New York Times**

FAST FACT: *At the 2012 Paralympics, McFadden and her sister Hannah, who runs track with a prosthetic left leg, became the first siblings to compete at the same Games.*

Who was the first athlete to win four world marathon majors in a year?

When she crossed the finish line at the 2013 New York City Marathon, **Tatyana McFadden** became the first person to win four of the six world marathon majors in one year, having also finished first in Boston, London, and Chicago. Through 2017, she had 21 major marathon victories, the most of any female wheelchair racer, and 17 Paralympic medals (seven gold, seven silver, and three bronze), including silver from the 2014 Winter Paralympics in cross-country skiing.

Born with a condition called spina bifida, McFadden is paralyzed from the waist down. She was adopted from a Russian orphanage when she was six and moved to the U.S. Thanks to lawsuits she filed while in high school in Maryland, disabled students must be included in that state's school athletic activities and be allowed to compete against able-bodied athletes.

FAST FACT:
Lopez won the New Mexico amateur tournament when she was 12 and the U.S. Girls' Junior Championship at 15 and again at 17.

Which golfer was the top rookie and player the same year she had the LPGA tour's lowest scoring average?

In 1978, 21-year-old **Nancy Lopez** announced her arrival to professional golf in grand fashion: She won five straight tournaments and nine total, including the LPGA Championship, and earned the tour's three major honors, still the only player to do so. "That year was a dream come true," she said.

Lopez became a popular star and an ambassador for the struggling LPGA. "She has been to the women's professional golf tour what

Billie Jean King was to women's tennis," wrote SPORTS ILLUSTRATED in 1979, "the individual who, because of her energy and skill, almost single-handedly brought widespread acceptance to a game previously regarded with indifference or contempt."

She was known for being an exceptional athlete and also for being exceptionally kind. After a quarter-century on the LPGA tour, she retired with 48 victories.

Who won the inaugural women's Olympic marathon?

The men's marathon has been included in the Olympics since the first modern Games, in 1896, but it wasn't until nearly a century later that women were granted a 26.2-mile event of their own. At the 1984 Games, **Joan Benoit Samuelson** of Maine was frustrated with the race's early pace and sped ahead of the pack in the first three miles. The other runners waited for her to fade, but she never did. "I took a chance," she said, "and I lucked out." Her time of 2:24:52 earned her gold by nearly 1½ minutes.

Who was the most recent two-time Olympic gold medalist in figure skating?

She landed her first triple jump when she was 11 years old and was a world and Olympic champion at 18. **Katarina Witt** skated with skill and grace, dominating the sport during the 1980s. Competing for East Germany, she joined Sonja Henie as the only other woman to ever defend an Olympic singles title (1984, 1988), and Witt won four of the five world championships held during that time. She also won six straight European championships, from 1983 through 1988. Like Henie before her, Witt was also an actress. "But the role I like best is of champion," said Witt.

109

Which U.S. hockey player has won nine world championship medals?

You've obviously done a little something special when your hometown celebrates a day in your honor. Indeed, hockey player **Hilary Knight** had won three world championships in four appearances, an NCAA championship at Wisconsin, and a silver Olympic medal when Sun Valley, Idaho, recognized her. May 19, 2011, was Hilary Knight Day. She was a star already, but over the next seven years, she would become one of the greatest women's hockey players in U.S. history. Knight won four more world championship gold medals and one silver, and was named MVP of the 2015 and 2016 tournaments. She scored 22 goals for the Boston Pride team that won the inaugural National Women's Hockey League title in 2016 and also scored twice to help Team USA win gold at the 2018 Olympics.

Which soccer player was named FIFA's female athlete of the 20th century?

She scored the first-ever goal for the U.S. women's national team in its first year of existence (1985), and she scored the game-winner in America's first-ever soccer world championship (the 1991 Women's World Cup). The 5'10" **Michelle Akers** was an imposing figure on the field and a figurative giant off it, an integral part of women's soccer's growth. "Our game is fast," she said in 1992. "It's fun. And when more people see women playing soccer at this level, they are going to get hooked." She was right!

WOW FACTOR

15

Fleming's age when she became the youngest U.S. women's figure skating champion.

Who was the last American to win three straight ladies' world figure skating titles?

C redited with ushering in the modern era of figure skating, **Peggy Fleming** won over America—and everyone else—with her elegance and stylishness on the ice in winning five consecutive U.S. titles starting in 1964, three straight world championships beginning in 1966, and the 1968 Olympic crown. She earned Team USA's only gold of those Games after finishing in sixth place in 1964, and she landed on the covers of LIFE and SPORTS ILLUSTRATED.

Leading up to the 1968 Olympics, her mother, Doris, spent a week furiously sewing six competition outfits from which her daughter could choose. Despite delivering a less-than-perfect routine that left her in tears, Fleming won convincingly over her rivals. "It was all rougher than I thought," she said afterward. "I mean, up until tonight I had figured the worst part of the whole thing came a week ago when I came out to practice. All my competitors came around and sat on the edge of the rink and just killed me with piercing looks. I got through that all right, but this was something else."

> " *There are lots of disappointments ...* **sometimes I fight against being human** *...but in overcoming these I learn, and that makes my life worthwhile."*
>
> **—in 1966, to SPORTS ILLUSTRATED**

Who scored the quickest goal in U.S. women's national team history?

Twelve seconds after the whistle blew to begin a U.S. women's national team Olympic qualifier in February 2016, **Alex Morgan** sprinted downfield, corralling a header from teammate Carli Lloyd and powering a kick into the back of the net past a stunned Costa Rica goalkeeper. It was believed to be the fastest goal scored in USWNT history.

U.S. Soccer has turned to Morgan as the leader of its next generation of stars, and she has embraced the challenge and attempted to raise the bar for American soccer athletes. Morgan became one of only a handful of U.S. players to compete overseas, helping French team Olympique Lyonnais win the 2016–17 UEFA Women's Champions League before returning home to play for the Orlando Pride of the National Women's Soccer League.

WOW FACTOR

81

Goals a 28-year-old Morgan had scored for the USWNT through January 2018, seventh on the all-time list.

DID YOU KNOW?

At the 2008 FIFA U-20 Women's World Cup, Morgan scored the winning goal in the final against North Korea *(above)*. She made her first appearance for the USWNT in March 2010 and scored her first goal that October. During her senior season at the University of California Berkeley, Morgan was called up again to play with the senior team during qualifying for the 2011 World Cup.

Which rower has won the most Olympic medals?

Not only was **Elisabeta Lipă** of Romania an incredible athlete, but she was also able to sustain her successful career for two decades, competing in six Olympics beginning in 1984 and bringing home at least one medal from each Games.

And she didn't just stick to one event. Lipă rowed with a partner in double sculls (gold, two silver), with three others in quadruple sculls (bronze), and by herself in single sculls (gold). She helped her country's women's eight boat win three times, becoming the oldest rower to claim gold in the event as a 35-year-old in 2000, then doing it again four years later as Romania beat the U.S. by nearly two seconds. Her grand total? Eight medals.

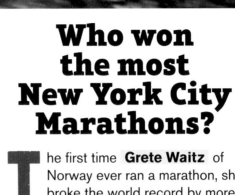

Who won the most New York City Marathons?

The first time **Grete Waitz** of Norway ever ran a marathon, she broke the world record by more than two minutes (2:32:30). That was at the 1978 New York City Marathon, and Waitz, a world-class runner at 3,000 meters and 10 kilometers, had completed only half of a marathon on her longest training run. It wasn't until after that unexpected New York win that she became serious about running the marathon. At the 1979 event, in fact, she beat her time by nearly five minutes to become the first woman to officially break 2½ hours at the distance (2:27:33). She won New York a record nine times.

Waitz was a role model to younger women in the world of distance running and beloved for her humility.

WOW FACTOR

6

Distances at which Waitz set world records: 3,000 meters, 8K, 10K, 15K, 10 miles, and the marathon.

Who is the most decorated Olympic tennis player of this century?

O ver a 16-year span, **Venus Williams** won an impressive five Olympic medals to tie for most in history among all tennis players. (Kathleen McKane of Great Britain won gold, two silvers, and two bronze in the 1920s.)

She kick-started her Olympic career in 2000 by being the first in 76 years to win singles and doubles at the same Games. Williams, of course, played doubles with sister Serena, and the duo won two more gold medals together.

Though the sisters didn't medal in women's doubles at the 2016 Games, Williams paired with Rajeev Ram, who plays on the ATP Tour, to win silver in mixed doubles and tie the record.

Through 2017, Williams also had seven Grand Slam singles titles.

Who scored gold-medal-winning goals for the U.S. women's soccer team in the 2008 and 2012 Olympics?

Casual soccer fans who tuned into the 2015 Women's World Cup final to see **Carli Lloyd** score a hat trick (three goals) in 16 minutes in Team USA's 5–2 win over Japan thought a star was emerging. The 32-year-old Lloyd's star, however, had been burning bright for quite some time.

This was the same player who had scored the lone goal in a 1–0 overtime win against Brazil in the 2008 Olympic gold medal game and who had scored both goals in a 2–1 win over Japan in the 2012 Olympic gold medal game.

This was also the same Lloyd who was cut from the U.S. Under-21 team and considered quitting the sport. "If you don't have difficult times, you don't learn or break barriers," she said after the 2015 World Cup win. "This journey has taught me so much."

After her big win in 1984, Retton became the first woman to appear on the front of Wheaties cereal boxes, which had for decades featured men. She rode in the Macy's Thanksgiving Day parade and appeared on the cover of *Seventeen* magazine—she was everywhere. America adored her. "I still think it's kind of neat," she said later that year of her instant fame. "I mean, I'd understand people recognizing me if I had purple hair or something, but I'm just a normal teenager. I'm still just Mary Lou."

Who was the first American woman to win the Olympic all-around?

The best that female U.S. gymnasts had ever fared at the Olympics was to earn bronze in the team event in 1948. Then along came 16-year-old **Mary Lou Retton,** performing in front of a boisterous crowd in Los Angeles at the 1984 Games. She needed to stick her vault, one of her strongest events, in order to win the all-around competition. She stuck it, all right: Retton scored a perfect 10 to clinch a victory, then landed another perfect 10 on her second run (which didn't even matter). "I knew I had it," she said later. "Listen: I knew by my run that I had it. I knew it when I was in the air!"

Along with Edwin Moses, America's 400-meter hurdler extraordinaire, Retton was named SPORTS ILLUSTRATED Sportsperson of the Year. "Well, nobody thought it could be done," she said of winning gold. "But you know what? I went and did it."

WOW FACTOR

5

Medals Retton won at the 1984 Olympics, more than any athlete there. She took silver in the team event and vault, and bronze in the uneven bars and floor exercise.

Which softball pitcher set an Olympic tournament record for batting average?

Yup. Batting average. **Lisa Fernandez** was so talented that she could pitch lights-out softball and deliver at the plate too. In high school she pitched a dozen perfect games. At UCLA she was named first-team All-America four times and the top player in the country three times. Her senior year, in 1993, she had both the lowest ERA in the NCAA (0.25) and the highest batting average (.510), and she is still second on the Division I career ERA list (0.22).

Fernandez was a big reason why the U.S. won the first three Olympic softball tournaments ever played; she pitched in all three gold medal games (1996, 2000, 2004). At the 2004 Olympics, she batted .545 to set a tournament record.

WOW FACTOR

25

Olympic record number of strikeouts Fernandez tossed in a 2000 game against Australia. (The U.S. lost in 13 innings.)

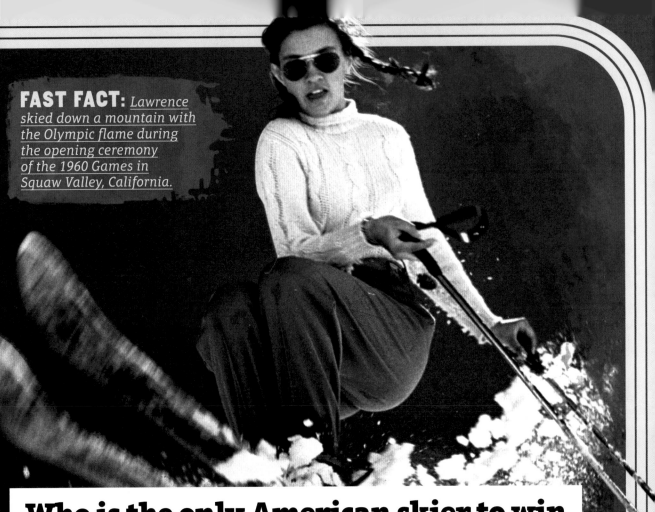

FAST FACT: *Lawrence skied down a mountain with the Olympic flame during the opening ceremony of the 1960 Games in Squaw Valley, California.*

Who is the only American skier to win two golds in a single Olympics?

Only 15 when she competed at the 1948 Olympics, **Andrea Mead Lawrence** finished eighth in the slalom, 21st in the combined event, and 35th in the downhill. She went on to win 10 of 16 races in 1951, including the event that served as an unofficial world championship. Lawrence arrived in Oslo, Norway, for the 1952 Games as the team captain, focused and determined. She hiked up and down the 1,000-meter giant slalom course, making mental notes about adjustments she should try. She won by more than two seconds, finishing in 2:06.8.

("Gee, that's good," she said afterward. "I didn't think I was going that fast.")

She fell twice during the downhill and didn't medal, and she took a tumble on her first slalom run. But she got back up and was in fourth place heading into the second and final run. She turned in the fastest time of the day by two seconds to win slalom gold by eight-tenths of a second.

Later in life, she became a conservationist, founding environmental organizations such as the Andrea Lawrence Institute for Mountains and Rivers.

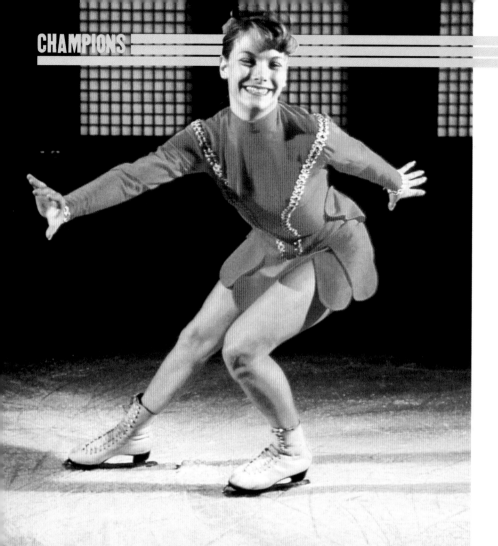

Who was named Canadian athlete of the 20th century?

Nicknamed Tiger by her teammates for the tenacious way she tackled the slopes, **Nancy Greene** of British Columbia won the inaugural Alpine skiing World Cup, in 1967. She then earned silver in the slalom and gold in the giant slalom at the 1968 Olympics, winning the latter race by a record margin (2.68 seconds). She repeated as overall World Cup champion in 1968, and by the time she retired, she had 17 Canadian national titles as well. In November 1999, she was named the Canadian athlete of the century for her accomplishments as an athlete and as an advocate for her sport. She was appointed to the Canadian Senate in 2009.

Who won five consecutive world figure skating titles in the 1950s?

For three years, **Carol Heiss** of New York battled countrywoman Tenley Albright for the title of best in the U.S. and the world. Heiss finished second to Albright at three straight national championships, at the 1955 world championships, and at the 1956 Olympics. One month after those Games, however, Heiss prevailed at worlds, the first of five in a row at which she would win gold. (The next month Heiss lost the U.S. title to Albright but then won four in a row.)

The spotlight was all Heiss's at the 1960 Games, where the 20-year-old New York University junior won gold. A ticker-tape parade was held in New York City in her honor.

Who was named MVP in four straight WNBA Finals?

She was playing overseas when **Cynthia Cooper-Dyke** heard about a new league starting in the U.S., the WNBA. Already 34 years old when she joined the Houston Comets during the summer of 1997, she teamed up with Sheryl Swoopes and Tina Thompson to lead the franchise to the league's first four titles, winning Finals MVP each time. Cooper-Dyke was also named league MVP in 1997 and 1998, the only time (through 2017) that a player has won the award in back-to-back years. She retired after winning that fourth championship, in 2000, then returned to the WNBA for a brief stint at age 40. Cooper-Dyke was inducted into the Hall of Fame in 2010.

WOW FACTOR

2

NCAA titles USC won while she and future Hall of Famer Cheryl Miller were on the team in the mid-1980s.

125

PLAYER INDEX

WOMEN ATHLETES WHO RULE!

PHOTO CREDITS